CHRISTIANS
TODAY
—QUESTIONS—
CHOICES WE MAKE !

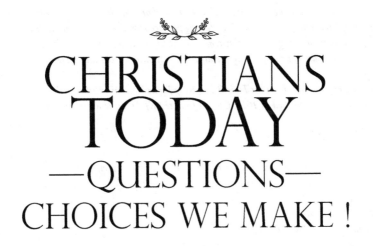

CHRISTIANS TODAY
—QUESTIONS—
CHOICES WE MAKE !

CHARLES PHILLIPS

CHRISTIANS TODAY—QUESTIONS—CHOICES WE MAKE!

Scripture quotations from the Holy Bible, King James Version (Authorized Version). First published in 1611. Quoted from the KJV Classic Reference Bible.

iUniverse books may be ordered through booksellers or by contacting:

iUniverse
1663 Liberty Drive
Bloomington, IN 47403
www.iuniverse.com
1-800-Authors (1-800-288-4677)

ISBN: 978-1-5320-7592-6 (sc)
ISBN: 978-1-5320-7593-3 (e)

Library of Congress Control Number: 2019906282

Print information available on the last page.

iUniverse rev. date: 06/24/2019

CONTENTS

INTRODUCTION

The Holy Scriptures is the oldest history Book we have today. Starts when the world was created by God and gives the history of nations that were, and those today. We know from God's Holy Word; Bible", the history of Creation, how God created the heavens and the earth, the light, the water, and dry land. He created the grass, herbs, fruit trees. God divided the day from the night, then signs and seasons, for days and years. He put lights in the firmaments of the heavens to give light on the earth. Light to rule the day, and the lesser light to rule the night, and he made the stars also. God then created an abundance of living creatures for the waters and birds to fly above the earth. God then created living creatures according to its kind, cattle, and everything that creeps on the earth. and God saw that it was good. God then made man in His own image, and put him in dominion over all He had made. God also created the woman. [Gen 1:1-31] God done all this in six days and said it was good.

[Gen 2:1-25] Tells that God finished all His work in six days and rested. The seventh day, God rested from all His work and blessed the seventh-day. That is the history of this earth, how it was made "created" and by Whom, all in seven days.

Like emigrants on a march to a heavenly land, God's people are traveling through this world to a much better place. To guide us on our journey, the Lord has provided land marks to encourage us to continue in the right direction. His Holy Scriptures reveals the way for us to know His Truth and know with certainly that we are on the right way and one day soon we will see our Lord come to take us home with Him. Do you want to be ready? Today is the day to decide!

The Church is God's appointed agency for the salvation of men. It is organized for service, and its mission is to carry the Gospel to all the world.

Passing by the self-righteous teachers, the Master Worker chose humble, unlearned men to proclaim the truths that were to move the world. Jesus ordained twelve men that He might send them forth to preach. It is seldom that one minister has all the requirements necessary to perfect a church in all the requirements of Christianity; therefore God sends to them other ministers, each possessing some qualification in which others were deficient.

Everyone who has received the Gospel has been given sacred truth to impart to the world. But though In this age there are many preachers, there is a great scarcity of able, holy ministers—men filled with the love that dwelt in the heart of Christ. Communion with God will impart to the minister's efforts a power greater than the influence of his preaching. The heart of the 'true' minister is filled with the intense longing to save souls.

In apostolic times, Satan led the Jews to exalt the ceremonial law and reject Christ; today he induces many professing Christians under pretense of honoring Christ, to cast contempt on the moral law and teach that its precepts may be transgressed with impunity.

If ministers of the gospel were to bear constantly in mind the fact that they are dealing with the purchase of the blood of Christ, they would have a deeper sense of the importance of their work. Some leaders and ministers are determined that the work of preaching the Gospel must be conducted in accordance with their own ideas. These men have lost sight of the fact that God is the teacher of His people. Let no one feel he is stepping down in becoming a child of God. Christ hung upon Calvary's cross, dying in our behalf, that we might have eternal life. Does it seem a small thing that He should endure all this, that we might be called the sons of God?

Does it seem a small thing to you to become members of the royal family, children of the heavenly King, partakers of the immortal inheritance?

The gospel has ever achieved its greatest success among the humbler classes. "Not many wise men after the flesh, not many mighty, not many noble, are called-1 Cor 1:26.

Beware lest any man spoil you through philosophy and vain deceit, after the traditions of men, after the rudiments of the world, and not after Christ.

To many, the Bible is a lamp without oil. Man is to regard the Bible as the voice of God speaking directly to him. Among professing ministers there are those who preach the opinions of men instead of the Word of God. Many among both ministers and people are trampling under their feet the commandments of God, and Satan laughs in triumph at the success of his devices. The growing contempt for God's law, there is an increasing distaste for religion, an increase of pride, love for pleasure, disobedience to parents. The only way to correct this is to preach God's Word—His commandments.

So long as we maintain our union with Christ, no one can pluck us out of His hand. Salvation is not earned by obedience, but is the fruit of faith and love.

The church is God's agency for the proclamation of truth. The great truth's necessary for salvation are made clear as noonday, and none will mistake and lose their way, except those who follow their own judgment instead of the plainly revealed will of God.

CHAPTER 1

CHRIST PEOPLE—CHRISTIANS— WHO ARE THEY?

The Bible is a system of revealed truths, so clearly given and simply given that a man or a fool need not era. We know that there are both Christian's and false Christian's in the church today and will be till Christ comes. It is not man's duty to separate, this will be done by God when He comes. We need to test all theories and doctrines we hear and read by the word of God. When others think you are wrong in your faith and practice of worship, have them show you from the word of God that you are in error from the Bible. Some may think that the message in Scripture is for the people in the time in which it was written. Like Noah's message before the flood which was true then, but only eight believed and was saved, today people are reluctant to believe also.

Why is the doctrine and preaching of Christ's second coming so unwelcome to our churches today? This great truth has become a stone of stumbling and a rock of offense to His people? The message of Christ coming should now be, as when made by the angels to the shepherds of Bethlehem, good tidings of great joy.

GOD created mankind, at the week of creation and mankind belongs to God, and created in the Image of God. Adam and Eve sinned in the garden of God, thus all the decedents of Adam and Eve have sinned. Satan claims that all mankind belongs to him since all have sinned. We can read in [Rev 22:14-15] "blessed are they that do His Commandments, that they may enter in through the gates into the City." God will have a people that believes and trust and worship as God has ask, but it's our choice. God does not force because in Love there is no "force." The choices we make in following Christ will determine our fate!

Christians today need to examine more carefully the foundation of our faith, and reject everything, however widely accepted by the Christian world, that is not founded upon the Word of God, "Scriptures."

CHAPTER 2

SIN—WHAT IS SIN—WHERE DID IT COME FROM, WHEN?

Lucifer was the first to sin when he wanted to be like Christ. He wanted to be greater than God. He said in [Isa 14:13-14] "I will ascend to the heavens, I will set up my throne above the stars of God. I will sit on the mount of the gods assembly, in the remotest parts of the North. I will ascend above the highest clouds; I will make myself like the Most High." Lucifer first sinned, then tempted Eve in the garden, and both Eve and Adam sinned and thus the whole earth is victim of sin.

The only definition of sin is that given in the Word of God; it is the transgression of Gods Law.[1John 3:4] [James 4:17] "Therefore to him that knoweth to do good, and doth it not, to him it is sin." [James 1:15] "—lust bringeth forth sin, when it is finished, bringeth forth death." God desires from all His creatures the service of Love. God takes no pleasure in a forced allegiance, and to all His creation, He grants freedom of will, that they may render Him voluntary service. Look at all His creations, they all have love in their beings. Consider the animals, does your pets, "dog or cat" render love to you? Even Lucifer, when created had Love, which he turned to himself rather than others. Do we see the same happening today in this world? What happens when people today pride themselves in selfish love? They usually lose their friends. God permitted Lucifer to carry forward his work, until the spirit of disaffection ripened into open rebellion. Even some of the Holy angels could not fully discern Lucifer's character, or see where his work was leading. They could not discern the consequences that would result from setting aside the divine Law. Had God in His justice and mercy destroyed Lucifer been immediately, all the angels and the worlds would have served God from fear, rather than love.

[Rom 5:13] "Sin is not imputed when there is no law." V-20 "for by the Law is the knowledge of sin." [Gal 5:14] "For all the Law is fulfilled in one word— 'love". Jesus said while on earth, [Matt 5:17] "Think not that I am come to destroy the Law or the prophets; I am not come to destroy, but to fulfill."

Mankind must remember that where there is no Law, there is no sin. Satan's claim was that angels needed no control-"Law"-but should be left to follow their own will. This same spirit that prompted rebellion in heaven, still inspires rebellion on earth today. Reproof of sin still arouses the spirit of hatred and resistance. From the day of Abel to our own time, such is the spirit that is displayed toward those who dare to condemn sin.

In the contest between Christ and Satan, during our Savior's earthly ministry, Satan demanded that Christ should pay him homage, when on the mountain summit, and the pinnacle of the temple and inspired the hearts of the priests and people to reject His love, and to cry out, "Crucify Him." It was and is Satan who prompts the world to reject Christ. Satan is still today exerting all his power to destroy Christ from the minds of people. Satan has revealed his true character as a liar and a murderer. The whole universe will become witnesses to the nature and results of sin.

God's Holy Law is a law of love, the foundation of His goverment. The death of Jesus Christ was an argument in man's behalf that could not be overthrown. The penalty of the law fell upon Christ who was equal with God, and man was free to accept the righteousness of Christ. Jesus not only came to accomplish the redemption of man, He came to magnify the "Law" and "make it honorable." It was to demonstrate to all the worlds that God's Law is unchangeable.

CHAPTER 3

WHY ARE SOME CHURCHES TODAY CALLED PROTESTANT CHURCHES?

During the first 2500 years of human history, there was no written revelation. those who had been taught of God, Adam and his decedents, communicated their knowledge of God to others, and this was handed down from father to son, through successive generations.

The preparation of the written word began in the time of Moses. This continued during the long period of 1600 years—from Moses, the historian of creation and the Law, to John, the recorder of the truths of the Gospel.

Satan was the first to transgress God's Holy Law. Satan led the Jews to reject Jesus Christ and today inspires people to reject the Word of God just as he did the Jews. The followers of Christ will tread the same path of humiliation, reproach, and suffering which the Master trod.

Satan, to more successfully war against God's church, has planted idolaters in the church to receive part of the Christian faith, while they reject essential truths. They accepted Jesus as the Son of God, and believed in His death and resurrection; but no conviction of sin, and feel no need of repentance. Most of the Christians consented to lower the standards, and the union was formed between Christianity and paganism. The pagans worshiped the Sun god and that was the beginning of Sunday worship.

The church today is not of a pure and holy character that marked the Christian faith in the days of Christ and His apostles. The church has substituted human theories and traditions in place of the requirements of God. This gigantic system of false religion is a masterpiece of Satan's power. Satan has as his leading doctrines of Romanism that the Pope is the visible head of the universal church of Christ, with supreme authority over bishops and pastors in all parts of the world. This is the same claim of Satan to Christ in the wilderness of temptation. God has never given a hint in His Word that He has appointed any man to be the head of the church.

In the first centuries, the true Sabbath had been kept by all Christians. Satan worked through his agents to bring about his purpose. Sunday thus was made a festival in honor of the resurrection of Christ. Religious services were held in honor of the resurrection of Christ; yet it was regarded as a day of recreation, the Sabbath being still observed as God's Sabbath. The bishop of the church urged the emperor to help unite the heathen and Christians and thus advance the power and glory of the church. God fearing Christians still held the true Sabbath as the Holy of the Lord, and observed it in obedience to the forth commandment.

The pagan festival came finally to be honored as a divine institution,while the Bible Sabbath was pronounced a relic of Judaism. thus the great apostate had succeeded in exalting himself -"above all that is called God, or that is worshiped-[2 Thess 2:4]. Protestants now urge that the resurrection of Christ on the first day of the week "Sunday" made it the Christian Sabbath, but Scripture evidence is lacking.

It was the Waldenses, Luther, Wycliffe and others that planted the seeds of Truth from God's Bible that is carried forward till today and will be carried forward till the close of time. John Wycliffe saw in his studies of Scripture that Rome had forsaken the Word of God for human traditions, and demanded that the Bible be restored to the people, and its authority be established in the church. More that forty years after his death his Bones were exhumed from the grave and publicly burned, and the ashes were thrown into a brook. Little did they know or realize the significance of their malicious act. As the water carried his ashes into the water of the ocean's so would the Gospel go to all the world. Many of the reformers died in the flames, and their execution exhibited to the whole world the cruelty of Rome. Of all those who led the church from popery into the light of a purer faith, stood Martin Luther. He acknowledged no foundation for religious faith but the Scriptures. Opposition is the lot of all whom God employs to present truths applicable to their time. Those who present truth for this time should not expect to be received with greater favor than were earlier reformers. Those who preach the Word of God in its purity will be received with no greater favor now than then. The Gospel is now, as in former times, a cause of trouble and dissension. Jesus said while on earth 'I came not to send peace on the earth, but a sword.' The gospel of Christ cannot be preached without offense. Satan seeks to divert men's thoughts from God, and fix them on human traditions.

It was the protest of believers during the "Reformation" for "Truth" that the name "Protestant" was given to the Reformers and believers of the Scriptures "Bible" in 1529. There is a wide departure from the doctrines and truth, and there needs to be a return to the Bible, and the Bible only as the rule of faith and duty. It is not as communities but as individuals that men are converted to God.

It was this time when these reformers were preaching truth from the Bible that Rome created the order of Jesuits, the most cruel and powerful of all the champions of popery. Rome vowed to over throw Protestantism and reestablish the papal supremacy. The most intellectual and highly educated and devoted pastors, were slain or forced to flee to other lands. To pray to God in secret and to refrain from bowing to an image, or sing a psalm, was punishable with death.

At this time in history, the right of every person to worship God according to the dictates of his own conscience was not acknowledged. Many were driven across the ocean to America, and here laid the foundation of civil and religious liberty which has been the glory of this country.

The year 1054, the Catholic Church and the Orthodox Church split. From the Catholic Church many other Churches developed. 1517 the Lutheran —and from the Lutheran's

1525 the Anabaptists-

1530-Hutterite—

1536-Calvinists (Reformed)—Presbyterians

1537-Mennonite,-usa-1725

1693-Amish.—

1885-Lutheran— EVANGELICAL COVENANT—1950— Evangelical Free.

1607—Congregationalists

1801—Churches of Christ

1844—Adventist-Baptist

1845—Southern Baptist

1863—Seventh-day Adventist

1915—National Baptist

1924—American Baptist and others

From the Catholic Church

1534—Episcopal—Anglicans

1738—Methodists—1814—African   Methodists—1890— Plymouth Brethren—

1887—Christian Missionary Alliances

1908—Church of the Nazarene.

1901—Pentecostals

1886—Church of God

1907—Pentecostal Assemblies

1914—Assemblies of God

1927—Foursquare Gospel

Charismatic

1965—Calvary Chapel

1983—Vineyard Ministries

From all the different groups or Churches, you can see how the name PROTESTANT name came about. Each group was a protest against the Roman Church that dictated what was to be understood by people. Each group of believers with, what they understood, wanted to be grouped together.

The religion which is current in our day is not of the pure and Holy Character that marked the Christian faith in the days of Christ and His Apostles.

There are over 500 Sabbath keeping Churches of all different denominations. The hundreds of different Sabbath keeping Churches that know the blessings of keeping God's Sabbath do not keep the day to earn entrance into the Kingdom but keep the day because they Love God with all their heart, soul and might. Salvation is a free gift and so there is nothing we can do to earn our salvation or entrance into the Kingdom as we are justified by faith and not by works of the Law. but does this mean we do not need to obey God's law? Thankfully, Paul made the answer to this question clear and informs us that we do not make void the Law through faith— Rom 3:31.

Sabbath keeping Churches know that keeping the Sabbath day is a sign that it is God we love and worship and that we are His children. Even though we cannot earn our way into the kingdom by keeping the Ten Commandments, we are still judged by them, and will not make it into the kingdom by not trying to keep them all in love and obedience to God. 1John 2:4—"He that saith, I know Him, and keepeth not His commandments, is a liar, and the truth is not in him. Sabbath keeping churches also know that God said we are to call His Holy day a delight, not legalism.

This gigantic system of false religion is a master piece of Satan's power. Satan to maintain his power over men, and establish the authority of the papal power, he must keep people in ignorance of the Scriptures. For hundreds of years the circulation of the Scriptures was prohibited. It was the protest of believers during the "Reformation for Truth in the Bible that gave the name "Protestant", was given to the reformers and believers of the Scriptures in the year 1529.

CHAPTER 4

IS THE GOSPEL TRUTH NOW, AS IN FORMER TIMES, A CAUSE OF TROUBLE AND DISSENSION?

The Gospel of Christ cannot be preached without offense. Satan seeks to divert men's thoughts from God, and fix them on human agencies for Truth. The great sin charged against Babylon is, "she has made all nations drink of the wine of the wrath of her fornication." The false doctrines that churches have accepted and been taught from Rome, rather than the Scriptures, has tied up what they are to preach. The religious faith of the churches of Rome appear so confused and discordant, that people don't know what or who to believe as Truth. Those who base their faith upon a personal knowledge of the Bible, will be like a rock and will not be moved by what the world believes. Each one of us must stand for the truth. The Lord does not save churches, only those who Love Him. No person is proved to be a Christian because he is found in company with the children of God, even in the house of worship. Many who pretend to be followers are following the traditions of men, and are as ignorant of truth as others who make no such pretensions of Christianity.

People today have only one way to judge when we hear our preachers and teachers speak or teach about the Gospel of Truth.

This is found "Isa 8:16,20" If they speak not according to this word, it is because there is no light in them."

The world today is at the same point as was the people were before the flood. People reasoned, how could so many people be wrong when they had never seen rain. Only Noah believed God, and was saved from the flood waters. What does the world believe today? Most only believe and choose what they want, of the Law of God. What will be their end? Today as in Noah's day, Religion has become the sport of infidels and skeptics because many are ignorant of its principles. The power of godliness has well-nigh departed from many churches. Picnics, church theatricals, church fairs, fine houses, personal display have banished thoughts of God. Things of eternal interest receive hardly a passing notice.

Satan can present a counterfeit so closely resembling the truth that it deceives those willing to be deceived, but impossible for Satan to hold under his power one soul who honestly desires to know the Truth.

Many today rest their hope on the authority of Satan, and is echoed from the pulpits of Christendom, and received by the majority of mankind as readily as it was received by Eve and Adam.

It is Satan's constant effort to misrepresent the character of God, the nature of sin in the great controversy. Satan causes people to regard God with fear and hate, rather than with love. Protestantism has so greatly degenerated since the days of the reformers, that there is little difference that exists today between churches. From the very beginning of the great controversy in heaven, it has been Satan's purpose to overthrow the Law of God. Many ministers are teaching their people, and many professors and teachers are instructing their students, that the law of God has been changed. the christian world strikes more boldly against the authority of Heaven with their teaching that the Law of God is no longer binding upon men, than anytime in history. Every nation has laws and how can any person conceive that the Creator of the heavens and the earth has no law to govern the beings He made? How long would the ministers be tolerated if they publicly taught that the laws of the land today are not obligatory, that they restricted the liberties of it's people, therefore ought not to be obeyed. How long would such men be tolerated in the pulpits? Is it a graver offense to disregard the laws of states and nations than upon the divine Law, the foundation of all Laws and government? Can you imagine what this world would be like without laws?

Why do we hear today, that the Law of God was nailed to the cross and made void? To destroy faith in the Bible serves Satan's purpose as well as to destroy the Bible itself. It is one of Satan's devices to combine falsehood with just enough truth, to give it plausibility. Nothing can justify setting aside the commandments of God for the precepts of men.

The Christian world has shown contempt for the Law of God,; and the Lord will do just as He declared that he would,—He will withdraw His blessings from the earth, and remove His protecting care from those rebelling against His Law. Satan has control of all whom God does not guard. We see today the results; fierce tornadoes, hail storms, floods, cyclones, tidal waves, and earthquakes, in every place where Satan is exercising his power. These things are to become more and more frequent and disastrous. The great deceiver 'Satan' will persuade men that those that serve God are causing these disasters. Satan seeks to destroy those who honor God's Law and will seek to destroy them, that's the difference, God never forces our will or conscience, but Satan through fear and force, endeavors to rule the conscience to secure homage to himself.

The opponents of Jesus while on earth were men whom the people had been taught from childhood. It was these Jewish leaders and teachers who refused to search the Scriptures concerning the truths for that time and taught what they thought was right. [Prov 16:25] "There is a way that seemeth right unto man, but the end therefore are the ways of death." Do we hear and see this today. Ignorance is no excuse for error or sin, when there is opportunity to know the will of God. It is not enough to have good intentions, or do what a man thinks is right or what the minister says. Our soul's at stake, search the Scriptures for yourself, comparing scripture with scripture. We will answer for our selves before God. Not one person is to suffer the wrath of God until the truth has been brought home to his mind and conscience, and has been rejected. Everyone will have sufficient knowledge to make his decision. The gospel without the law is inefficient and powerless. The law and the gospel are a perfect whole and produce love and faith unfeigned.

The popular ministers, like the Pharisees of old, will denounce the message of Truth as of Satan, and stir up the sin-loving multitudes to persecute those who proclaim it. Obedience to the word of God will be treated as rebellion and will be persecuted for their faith. Some will experience the same trials as Wycliffe, Huss, Luther. No person can serve God without enlisting against himself the host of darkness. In the time of trial, every soul must stand for himself before God, as did Noah, Daniel, and Job.

CHAPTER 5

TRUTH

Are we able to believe Truth today more than when Christ walked among men on earth? [John 1:14] "The Word was made flesh, and dwelt among us—full of grace and Truth." V—17 "Grace and Truth came through Jesus Christ." [John 14:6] "I am the way, the Truth and the life." [John 18:37] "Everyone that is of the Truth heareth My voice."

The Christians, when Christ walked the earth were no different than we today, Why? [Rom 1:25] "They exchanged the Truth of God for a lie, and worshiped and served something created instead of the Creator." We are told what the end will be for those who disobey the Truth [Rom 2:8] "Wrath and indignation to those who are self-seeking and disobey the truth." [2 Cor 4:4] "The god of this world hath blinded the minds of them which believe not, lest the light of the Glorious gospel of Christ, should shine unto them." [2Cor 13:8] "For we can do nothing against the Truth, but for the Truth." Paul asked the people to whom he preached [Gal 4:16] "Am I therefore become your enemy, because I tell you the Truth?" [Eph 1:13] "We should trust in the word of Truth, for the word of Truth is the gospel of our salvation, we are sealed with the Holy Spirit of promise. [Eph 5:6] "Let no man deceive you with vain words; for because of these things cometh the wrath of God upon the children of disobedience." [Eph 6:14] "Stand there-for, with Truth, like a belt around your waist, righteousness like armor on your chest." [2 Thess 2:10-11] "They perish because they did not accept the love of the Truth in order to be saved—. Christ desires [1 Tim 2:4] "all men to be saved and come to the knowledge of the truth."

We are warned in Scripture [2 Tim 3:1-2,7] "In the last days serious times will come; men will be lovers of self—having the form of godliness but denying its power— —always learning and never able to come to the knowledge of the Truth." [2 Tim 4:4] "They will turn their ears away from the truth and be turned aside to fables."

[1John 1:6] "If we say that we have fellowship with Him, and walk in darkness, we lie and do not practice the Truth." Many people today think they are worshiping our Creator God, they think they know God. How can we know for sure that we know and that we are serving God? Scripture tells us [2 John 2:3-5] "By this we know that we know Him, if we keep His commandments. He who says 'I know Him, and does not keep His commandments is a liar, and the 'truth' is not in him. But whoever keeps His word, truly the love of God is perfected in him. By this we know that we are in Him." John says that what we do, and not what we say tells the Truth about us. [1 John 3:18] "Let us not love in word or tongue, but in deed and in truth."

This generation today is no different than in John's day, or when the Scriptures were written. John says in [2 John 4] I have found some of your children walking in Truth, as we received commandment from the Father." [V-6] "This is love, that we walk according to His commandments. This is the commandment, that as you have heard from the beginning, you should walk in it."

Where do we find God's Truth for today? Do we hear from the pulpits? Do we read it from what someone has written, who has been trained in schools of Theology? There are many who think they preach the Truth but do they understand the Truth as it is written in God's Bible? How many churches, claim to know and preach God's Truth? There is [563] different Sabbath keeping denotations known today. Each claims to have the true message from Scripture for people. How many Sunday keeping churches are their today? Some of these claim to be only New Testament churches, who believe that the Old Testament was for the Jews only. What do these believers do when they come to one of the [250] quotations, but the number jumps to more than 1000, in the New Testament from the Old Testament? "It is used over 70 times in the New Testament, referring to what is written in the Old Testament.

God has preserved all the Truth that we need to come to the knowledge of His Love and repent and Christ will honor those that love and honor His Truth. God will not force anyone to come to Him. God will only take those who love Him, home to heaven to live eternal with others who know the Love of God.

CHAPTER 6

QUESTIONS?

Does it seem a small thing that Jesus should endure, stepping down from heaven to be hung upon Calvary's cross, die for our "sins" that we may become members of the royal family of heaven? Do people today believe in the Gospel and that Jesus Christ suffered to redeem those who believe?

Jesus once stood in age just where you stand today. Jesus had every temptation you and I have ever had. Many who are seeking for happiness will be disappointed in their hopes, because they seek it of their own. Many have confused faith and feelings. Do not think that because you have made mistakes you will always be under condemnation. The Bible says, "If we confess our sins, He is faithful and just to forgive us our sins, and to cleanse us from 'all' unrighteousness 1John 1:9. When truth and love takes possession of the heart, the Christian will be brought into conflict. "Temptation" is not sin, the sin lies in yielding.

Christ paid the ransom with His own life for every son and daughter of Adam for eternity. Christ has a claim upon every soul; but many choose a life of sin. Some say "I go, or I love, to Christ invitation; but they refuse, or they do not make a complete surrender. [Rev 3:8] Jesus says "Behold, I have set before thee an open door, and no man can shut it." This is His invitation for anyone to come to Christ, for help in the conflict in life. You and I must have help from above to resist the temptations of Satan and escape his devices. prayer is a privilege. We must have help which God alone can give, but that help will not come if we don't ask. Often the angels wait in vain, because we do not ask for the blessings of God.

Every repetition of sin weakens the power of resistance, blinds the eyes, and stifles conviction. The Lord sends us warning, counsel, and reproof, that we may have opportunity to correct our errors, before they become second nature. But if we refuse to be corrected, God does not interfere.

Religion will prove to you an anchor. Communion with God will impart to every holy impulse a vigor that will make the duties of life a pleasure. [Prov 6:6] "Go to the ant, thou sluggard, consider her ways, and be wise." Idol-ness, like a stagnant pool is offensive; but a pure, flowing spirit spreads health and gladness. We may profess what we will, but unless our lives corresponds with our profession, our faith is dead. Words and actions plainly testify what is in the heart.

CHAPTER 7

IS THE NUMBER SEVEN [7] SPECIAL TO JESUS CHRIST?

From the beginning God created the earth and all that was in it in seven-7-days.

Noah was on dry ground 'in the boat' seven-7-days before the rain began!

Israel marched around Jericho seven-7-days, and on the 7th day seven times.

Nanman the leper dipped in the river -7-times and was healed.

David and Bathsheba's baby died when seven-7-days old.

Samson had seven-7-locks of hair.

Soloman's temple was built in seven-7-years.

Elijah's servant looked for rain clouds seven-7- times on Mt Carmel.

Elisha told Israel the famine would last seven-7-years.

Elisha warmed the body of the Shumemite woman's son and the boy sneezed seven-7-times and lived.

Jehoash was seven-7-years old when he began to reign.

Jesus took seven-7-loaves of bread and fed 4000 people.

There are seven-7-churches addressed in the New Testament.

There are seven-7-stars addressed in Scripture.

There are seven-7- candlesticks addressed in Scripture.

Enoch was the seventh -7th- from Adam-Jude 1:14

The Lord destroyed seven-7-nations of Cannon—Acts 13:19

In prophecy God used a Lamb with seven-7- horns and seven-7-eyes—Rev 5:5.

In prophecy God used —seven-7-angels; seven-7-seals; seven-7-trumpets —Rev 8:1

God uses seven-7-angels to deliver seven-7- last plagues—Rev 15:1

Jesus spoke seven-7-times while on the cross.

Luke 23:34—To the Roman soldiers and the crowd looking on.

Luke 23:43—To the repentant thief on the cross beside Him.

John 19:26-27—To His Mother.

Matt 27:46—To His Father in heaven.

John 19:28—To the Roman soldier—"I Am thirsty"!

John 19:30—To the world "It is finished."

Luke 23:46—To His Father.

The Bible declares that creation occupied seven days. [Gen 1:1-5] "In the beginning God created the heavens and the earth. And the earth was without form and void; and darkness was upon the face of the deep. And the Spirit of God moved upon the face of the waters. And God said, let there be light. And God saw the light, that it was good; and God divided the light from the darkness. And God called the light Day, and the darkness He called Night. And the evening and the morning were the first day. This is the foundation of all Truth. Everything starts here. In Heb 11:3,6, we read: "Through faith we understand that the worlds were framed by the Word of God, so that things which are seen were made of things which do appear—but without faith it is impossible to please Him; for he that cometh to God must believe that He is, and that He is a rewarder of them that diligently seek Him.

The seven days of creation were not long periods of 500million years each as some would have you believe. The first seven days of time composed the first week. In fact there is no other origin for the week, or for a recruit period of seven days. You see, the week, composed of seven days, is itself a proof that the days of creation were seven literal days as we have them today.

How can we be sure that the days of creation were days of 24 hours. How long is a day? When the earth was made it started to rotate upon its axis from west to east, consuming in one revolution 23hours, 56 minutes, 4.09 seconds to be exact. This is the solar day.

According to the Bible, a record of time was kept, and that time was divided into years, months, weeks, and days just as we have them today, We can read in Gen 7:11: In the six hundredth year of Noah's life, in the second month, the seventeenth day of the month, the same day were all the fountains of the great deep broken up, and the windows of heaven were opened." So you see they kept a record of the years and months and days in Noah's time. Every month was composed of 30 days. the flood began when Noah was 600 years old—in the second month and on the seventeenth day of the month. This is a definite date and proves that records were kept. We can read in [Gen 8:22] "While the earth remaineth, seedtime and harvest, and cold and heat, and summer and winter, and day and night shall not cease."

Fascinating, about the number seven and how lots of things are divisible by seven-[7]-.

For example—the eggs of the potato bug hatch in seven-7-days.

—those of the canary in 14 days.

—those of the barnyard hen in 21 days

—those of the ducks and geese 28 days.

—those of the mallard duck 35 days.

—those of the parrot and ostrich 42 days.

all are divisible by seven, the number of days in a week.

CHAPTER 8

NOW ABOUT THE NUMBER SIX [6].

Ex 20:9—Six- 6- days you shall labor and do all your work.

Ex 20:11—Six-6- days the Lord made the heavens and the earth, the sea, and rested the 7th day.

Ex 23:12—six days you shall do all your work and rest the seventh, your ox, donkey, servant, &stranger.

Matt 27:45—from the sixth hour until the ninth hour, darkness covered the land.

The lives of each person may be ordered by the Lord in a beautiful way for His glory, if you will only trust Him with your life. If you try to regulate your own life, it will only be a mess and a failure. Only the One Who made the brain and heart can successfully guide them to a profitable end.

CHAPTER 9

WHAT IS GOD'S PURPOSE FOR HIS CHURCH?

The church is God's appointed agency for the salvation of mankind. It's mission is to carry the Gospel to all the world. Christ has said in [Isa 49:16] "I have graven thee upon the palms of My hands." The church is God's fortress, His city of refuge, which He holds in a revolted world. Any betrayal of the church is treachery to Him who has bought mankind with the blood of His only begotten Son.

Through centuries of persecution, conflict and darkness, God has sustained His Church. All His purposes will be fulfilled. His Law is linked with His throne, and no power of evil can destroy it or even any part of it.

The church is the theater of His Grace, in which He delights to reveal His power to transform hearts. Earthly kingdoms rule by the ascendancy of physical power; but Christ Kingdom is ruled by "Love" and every instrument of coercion is banished.

The Egyptian nation, God made Joseph a fountain of life. Through the integrity of Joseph, the life of that whole nation of people was preserved. Through Daniel, God saved the life of all the wise men of Babylon. These deliverances illustrate the spiritual blessings offered to the world through connection with God. God chose Israel to reveal His character to mankind. God desired Israel to be as wells of salvation in this world. To them was committed the laws of heaven, the revelation of God's will is for all people.

Most of the world, through corrupt practices, has lost the knowledge of God. The people of Israel lost sight of their high privileges as God's representatives. They robbed their fellow men of religious guidance and a holy example. They were satisfied with a legal religion, and it was impossible for them to give to others living Truths of heaven. The faith that works by love and purifies the soul could find no place in the religion of the Pharisees, made up of ceremonies and the injunctions of men.

As Israel of old failed in the mission that God had purposed, that the world would come to know Him, He turned to His disciples to carry on His work as He had hoped Israel would do. Christ did not choose the "learned or eloquence" of the Jewish or the power of Rome. He chose the humble, unlearned men to proclaim the Truths that can move the world.

The Bible is the only rule of faith and doctrine. Only Bible truth and Bible religion will stand the test of judgment. We are not to prevert the word of God to suit convenience, and worldly interests. We are not to be influenced from God's Truth by great and professedly good people as they urge their ideas above the plain statements of truth in the word of God. The enemy of all righteousness has taken the world captive and led men and women to disobey the law of God. Many among both ministers and people are trampling under their feet the commandments of God. The Creator of this world is insulted, and Satan laughs in triumph at the success of his devices. With this growing contempt for God's Law there is an increasing distaste for religion, an increase of pride, love of pleasure, disobedience to parents. What can be done to correct these alarming evils? As an educating power the Bible is without a rival. "The mind gradually adapts itself to the subjects upon which it is allowed to dwell."

The Bible came fresh from the fountain of eternal Truth, and has been preserved in purity through all the ages. The Bible is the most ancient and the most comprehensive history that we have. Here only do we find an authentic account of the origin of nations.

When unpopular Truths are presented, many refuse to make an effort of investigation to find Truth. To every soul will come the searching test; Shall I obey God rather than man? It is impossible for people to honor God by erroneous opinions. When the lawyer came to Jesus with the question "What shall I do inherit eternal life." Jesus told the lawyer "What is written in the Law?" Jesus makes answers so easy to understand that no one can say, I didn't understand. Make a choice today before its to late.

CHAPTER 10

JESUS, GOD'S GIFT TO MANKIND!

The plan for man's redemption was not an after thought of God and Christ, after the fall of Adam and Eve. [Rom 16:25 RV.] From the beginning, God and His Son knew of the apostasy of Satan, and the fall of man. God did not ordain that sin should exist.

Adam could have been made without free choice. He could have been made to worship God without free choice. He could have been made to worship God without knowing about Love. We know from through out Scripture that the kingdom of God is about Love, for God and our fellow man. The gift of Jesus Christ reveals the Father's heart of Love. While God's hatred of sin is as strong as death, His love for the sinner is stronger than death. God, having under taken our redemption, He spared nothing, however dear. No truth essential to our salvation is withheld, no miracle of mercy is neglected. The whole treasury of heaven is open to those He wants to save.

At the cross of Calvary, love and selfishness stand face to face. Putting Christ to death, Satan manifested the malignity of his hatred against God. Satan's real purpose was to dethrone God and destroy Jesus whom the love of God was revealed.

Jesus came with the Truth of heaven, and all who are listening to His voice are drawn to Him. The worshipers of self belong to Satan's kingdom. Our attitude toward Christ and His Law, show on which side we stand. And thus we all pass judgment on ourselves.

People today can see what happens when the Lord's Law of Love is disregarded. All those who refuse to give themselves to God and His Law of Love are under the control of another power. In the work of redemption there is no compulsion. It's our choice. The Law of God sets us free from the law of sin and death [John8:36; Rom 8:2]. The only condition upon which our freedom is possible is that of becoming one with Christ.—"The Truth shall make you free" John 8:32. God is Love, He does not force, its our choice whom we will love and obey. What will it be for you? God's way of love or Satan's way that leads to death? Decide now, talk to our Creator God today, ask Him to help you love Him.

CHAPTER 11

SHOULD PEOPLE TODAY HONOR THE LAW OF GOD?

What is the Law of God? Where in Scripture is God's Law? Why should we honor His Law today? The Law of God was given personally from God to Moses on Mt Sinai. It was a copy of the Law of God in heaven. How do we know? [Heb 8:2] "the true tabernacle which the Lord erected, and not man." The Law of God was handed to Moses by God on Mt Sinai, which was a copy of the Law in the tabernacle in heaven. God wrote His law on stone, that it could not be altered. This Law of God is the Law which all heaven honor's forever.

[Heb 8:5] "Moses was divinely instructed when he was about to make the tabernacle." [Rev 11:19] "Then the temple of God was opened in heaven, and the ark of the covenant was seen in the temple. [Rev 15:5] "After these things I looked, and behold the temple of the tabernacle of the testimony in heaven was seen." What is the Law and where do we find the Law of God that all heaven lives by and God wants us people on earth to live by? This Law of God is found in Exodus 20:3-17, and found through out Scripture. This is the only Law in Scripture given to mankind by God. Jesus explains in [Matt 22:36-40] that all the commandments hang on the main two commandments; "Love to God and love for our fellow man." The ten commandments are the only Laws written by God for mankind.

Why would Jesus Christ come to this world, that would not honor Him or follow His Law? Jesus answer's this in "John 3:16" Today we have one source that tells us how and why we are living the life we are here today. The one source we have is God's Holy Bible. Paul stated in [Rom 15:4] that what is written is for our instruction, to give us hope. We hear lots of false witness's today, but God has said in [Heb 6:18] "It is impossible for God to lie."

Why do Christians today call themselves Christians and honor not the Law of God? We have heard for years by those who claim to be preachers of God's Word, that the Law of God was nailed to the cross. we are also told many times and many places in Scripture that there are false teachers and prophets who teach and deceive the people of God. A few of the text that tell us about these are [Matt 7;15—Matt 15:14—Matt 23:3,5,28—Matt 24:24—Rom 10:2]—many more. Don't be fooled by popular people in this world! Remember Noah and the world then, how popular was Noah? Most of the people then did not believe what God said. Remember Lot, and Sodom, how many believed the angel and came to Lot? If you think Satan could tempt Adam and Eve in the garden of God, do you think he can deceive people today? Don't be deceived by Preachers and teachers that don't know the Scriptures! Very few knew or understood Scripture when Christ walked among men while on earth. Is it better today? Read and study God's Word "Bible" for yourself. You may not understand all you read, but ask God to help you to understand and know that His Law was not nailed to the cross with Christ. If the Law was nailed to the cross, then there would be no sin for we are told in [1John 3:4] "Everyone who commits sin also breaks the law; sin is the breaking of the law." [Acts 3:20]"for through the law comes the knowledge of sin," [1 Peter 4:14]'If you are ridiculed for the name of Christ, you are blessed." [1 John 2:4-5] "The one who says, I have come to know Him," without keeping His commandments, is a liar, and the truth is not in him. But whoso keepeth His Word, in him verily is the love of God perfected."

The question today is —Should Christians honor God's Law or just honor the parts that are popular in the Christian world today? [2John 6] "This is Love, that we walk according to His commandments." [2 Cor 5:21] "He made the One who knew not sin to be sin for us, so that we might become righteousness of God in Him." [Matt 7:22-23] "There will be many who will say to Me Lord, Lord, didn't we prophecy in Your name, drive out demons in your name, and do miracles in Your name?" "Then I will announce to them, 'I never knew you! Depart from Me, you lawbreakers." Will you or I be one of those who hear those words? Please, don't pick and choose the commandments that you like and ignore the commandments that the world choose's to ignore. God the Father gave all, His only Son to show His Love for all the people of this world.

CHAPTER 12

IS OBEDIENCE TO GOD'S LAW—LEGALISM?

We may think we can get away with violating traffic laws or cheating on taxes, but God and His Laws work much differently. God hears and sees everything we do, everything we say. Our Lord offers forgiveness for our sins, yet; there are still deadly consequences for breaking God's law. Some Christians think any attempt to obey God's Law is legalism. Jesus says in Scripture "If you really love God, you'll do what He asks. So is obedience legalism or love? [Gen 16:13] God has perfect knowledge of all we are or do. [Ps 139:1-4] Even the hairs of our head are numbered. [Luke 12:7] Not one word, thought, or deed is hidden from Him. Will we or can we be saved if we refuse to obey His Word? [Matt19:17] "If you want to enter into life, keep the commandments." [Heb 5:9] "He became the author of eternal life to those who obey Him."

Why does God require obedience and is it necessary? Our God of the universe is one God, with one Law for all the universe. The Bible is not merely advice which we can accept or ignore without consequences. We might ask, "Why" does God permit disobedience? The kingdom of God is a kingdom of Love only. Want you be thankful to be part in a kingdom where sin cannot exist? All people will finally realize that God, by requiring obedience, is not trying

33

to force His will upon us, but is trying to keep us from hurting and destroying one another.

Will God actually destroy the disobedient? [2 Peter 2:4] "God did not spare the angels who sinned, but cast them down to hell—to be reserved for judgment."[Ps 145:20] "All the wicked will be destroyed." It is not safe for people today to depend on our notions and feelings of what is right or wrong. Our only safety is depending on The Word of God.

We may ask, does God count man guilty for disobeying Bible Truth, that has never been made plain to him? [John 9:41\ "If you were blind, you would have no sin; but now you say 'we see' therefore your sin remains." [James 4:17] "To him who knows to do good and does not do it, to him it is sin." It is our responsibility to search for truth. Is it best to wait till all obstacles are gone before embracing Truth? It is never best to wait, procrastination is the devil's most dangerous trap. God says-"You go forward, and I will open the way."

Isn't full obedience an impossibility for human beings? [Matt 19:26] "With God all things are possible." [Philippians 4:13] "I can do all things through Christ who strengthens me." None of us can obey in our own power, but through Christ we can and must. Isn't love more important than obedience? Jesus says -[John 14:23-24] "If anyone loves Me, he will keep My word—He who does not Love Me does not keep My words." [1 John 5:3] "This is the Love of God, that we keep His commandments. And His commandments are not burdensome." The Bible teaches us that true love to God cannot exist without obedience. A person cannot truly be obedient without love! When love and obedience are separated, they die.

What happens when a person continues to willfully and knowingly disobey God? We find the answer in [2 Thess 2:11] "And for this reason God will send them strong delusion, that they should believe the lie."

Many think that true freedom in Christ, releases them from obedience to the law. Does it? Like on earth today and the laws of the land; we have freedom when we obey the laws of the land, not free from obeying them. Disobedience always hurts a person and leads into the cruel slavery of the devil. [Prov 28:26] "He who trust in his own heart is a fool." We must give God credit for being wise enough to require some things of us we may not understand. It is folly for us, in our ignorance, to question God's leadership, even when we may not fully understand all His reasons.

Who is really behind all disobedience, and why? [Rev 12:9] "Satan—deceives the whole world." He knows that all disobedience is sin and that sin brings unhappiness, tragedy, alienation from God and eventual destruction. Satan's bitter hatred of Christ, he tries to lead every person into disobedience and destruction. We are all involved in this hatred of Satan and he wants all to disobey God and be lost.

Will any be lost that think they will be saved? [Matt7:21-23] "Not everyone that saith unto Me, Lord, Lord, shall enter the kingdom of heaven; but he that doeth the will of My Father which is in heaven. Many will say to Me in that day, Lord, Lord, Have we not prophesied in thy name? And in thy name cast out devils? And in thy name done many wonderful works? And then will I profess unto them, I never knew you; depart from Me, ye that work iniquity." [John 10:27] "My sheep hear My voice, and I know them, and they follow Me."

We ask what about people who haven't received the knowledge of God's Truth? Will they be lost? We are told in {John 10:16] "And other sheep I have which are not of this fold; them also I must bring, and they will hear My voice; and there will be one flock and one shepherd." Christ knows those who never heard the Truth, and had they heard, they would have followed and honored Christ's Truth.

Remember, obeying Gods laws and the laws of the Land, we can enjoy true freedom, as long as laws of the land do not disagree with God's Law.

CHAPTER 13

FAITH!

What is Faith? Webster's say faith is trust; unquestioning belief,trust. [James 2:26] Faith without works is dead." Faith then must have works or we are dead. Verbal faith is not enough; mental faith is insufficient. Faith must inspire action. Faith endures trials. Faith understands temptations. Faith will not merely hear and not do. Faith harbors no prejudice. Faith displays itself in works. Faith is more than knowledge. Faith is demonstrated by obedience. Faith responds to the promises of God. Faith controls the tongue. Faith gives us the ability to choose wisdom that is heavenly and to shun wisdom that is earthly. Faith produces separation from the world and submission to God. Faith provides us ability to resist the Devil and humbly draw near to God. Faith waits patiently for the coming of the Lord. There are thousands who believe in the Gospel and in Jesus Christ as the world's Redeemer, but they are not saved by that faith. The faith that justifies always produces first true repentance, and then good works, which are the fruit of that faith. There is no saving faith that produces good fruit.

James 1:3—Testing of your faith produces patience.

V-22—be doers of the word, and not hearers only, deceiving yourself.

V-25—The person who looks into the perfect law of liberty and continues in it—this one will be blessed.

James 2:5—God has chosen the poor of this world to be rich in faith and heirs of the kingdom to those who love Him.

James 2:10-11-Who ever stumbles in one point of the Law, he is guilty of all the Law.

V-12—all will be judged by the Law.

V-17—Faith that has no works is dead.

V 19—You believe that there is one God, You do well. Even the demons believe and "tremble."

V-24—a man is justified by works, and not by faith only.

V-26—Faith without works is dead!

James 4:17—To him who knows to do good and does not do it, to him it is sin.

James 5:15—The prayer of faith will save the sick, the Lord will raise him up—if he has committed sins, he will be forgiven!

CHAPTER 14

WHY OBEY AS GOD HAS ASKED?

It is not human nature to do what is right. Satan is the first to be the one to do as what he thought would be best for himself, then try to get others to think as he thinks. Do we see and hear the same today? The Lord is the Creator of all that is good and He knows what is best for all mankind. Satan began his controversy in heaven with the angels, telling them he had a better plan. We all can see today what his plan has developed into. Our Creator calls Satan's plan 'sin'! We people today, now see that if Satan's plan is allowed to continue, every one and everything will come to destruction and death. Satan's plan is to deny Christ of His work of Creation of mankind.

When Adam and Eve chose to disobey their Creator and do as they thought might be a better choice, so has mankind today! This carried on with Adam and Eve's children. The Lord told Adam and Eve and all that was to come after them to slay a lamb as an offering to the Lord. WHY? When Adam and Eve sinned by disobeying God, by eating of the fruit of the tree in the garden of God, then they saw what sin brings, fear and doubt. They hid from God or thought they had. God slew the first lamb for a covering for Adam and Eve, because of their sin, they saw that they were naked and were afraid. Sin brings fear and death, not only to mankind, but to all of God's creation on earth.

Why did God require Adam and Eve to slay a lamb for an offering of sacrifice? This was to be a reminder to all mankind that God was to one day, let His only begotten Son, 'Jesus Christ' come to this world and be sacrificed for the sins of every person that has been born and was to be born on earth.

When Adam and Eve chose to disobey God and do as they thought, thinking they had made a better choice, people are doing the same thing today! The children of Adam and Eve did the same when Cain thought he would offer a sacrifice of things from his garden. The Lord had told Adam and Eve to offer a Lamb, to slay the Lamb, and the blood from that lamb represented and pointed to the day when Jesus Christ who would come and be killed and sacrificed, His blood would cover our sins— "be forgiven"—blotted out of the book of remembrance.

Cain the brother of Able, when he offered his offering of sacrifice; is also happening today. Cain didn't want to do as God had planned for mankind, Cain wanted to substitute God's plan for his plan. What happened was that God did not accept Cain choice and this upset Cain and he was mad at his brother because God did not accept Cain's sacrifice, but accepted Able's. Cain then killed his brother and we see the same today. There are religious people in foreign country's that will today kill those who are worshiping their God and think they are doing what they should. Even in America we see this same attitude. People get upset when they think of people worshiping on the day God created for worship and not the day, mankind has chosen to worship.

What day have you and I chosen, God's Sabbath or man's sabbath? Have you chosen a day for the Sabbath or have you accepted God's Sabbath? I hope you and I will do as God has asked and not be a modern day Cain.

We are told in [Isa 66:22-23] "All flesh will come to worship before Me, from one Sabbath to another." There won't be, but one Sabbath in heaven. Why not start this week obeying and worship

God as He has invited all to worship. God is love and where love is, there is no harm, bitterness, hate, or any kind of evil.

Make your choice today and enjoy the blessings of God. Don't be like Cain, [Jude 11] "Woe to them! For they have gone in the way of Cain, have run greedily in the error of Balaam for profit and perished, in the rebellion of Korah."

CHAPTER 15

LOVE—WHAT IS LOVE?

What is Love? Can Love be explained? We read in [1John 4:8] "God is Love." [1 John 4:16] "God is love and he who abides in love abides in God, and God in him." [1 John 4:18] "There is no fear in love, but perfect love cast out fear, because fear involves torment." [Prov 10:12] "Love covers all sins."

How do we express Love?]1John 3:18] "Let us not love in word or in tongue, but in deed and in truth." [1John 4:7-8] "Beloved, let us love one another, for love is of God; and everyone who loves is born of God and knows God. he that does not love, does not know God for God is love." [V-20] "If someone says 'I love God and hates his brother, he is a liar."

We are told in [1John 3:13-16] "Do not marvel my brethren, if the world hates you. We know that we have passed from death to life, because we love the brethren. He who does not love his brother abides in death. He who hates his brother is a murderer, and you know that no murderer has eternal life abiding in him. By this we know love, because He laid down His life for us, and we also ought to lay down our lives for the brethren."

The best known verse in Scripture in all the world is [John 3:16]" For God so loved the world that He gave His only begotten Son, that whosoever believes in Him should not perish but have everlasting life." V-17—"For God did not send His Son into the world to condemn the world, but the world through Him might be saved." From these verses we understand that this world will one day end and some will not be saved.

We now need to find who will be saved and who will not be saved. Is there a way to know? Will I be one of those who will be saved? Is there a way for us to know if we will be saved? Look first at those who will not be saved. [Gal 5:19-21] "Those who are found in -'adultery, fornication, uncleanness, lewdness, idolatry, sorcery, hatred, contentions, jealousies, outbursts of wrath, selfish ambitions, dissensions, heresies, envy, murders, drunkenness, reveries, and the like; those who practice such things will not inherit the Kingdom of God."

We are told in [John 18:36] "My kingdom is not of this world." [Ps 145:13] "Your kingdom is an everlasting Kingdom."

One thing we know, God is a God of Love and His kingdom will be made up of those that know what love is and how to express love, [Rom 8:38-39] "Neither death nor life, nor angels nor rulers nor things present, nor things to come, nor powers, nor heights, nor depth, nor any other created thing will have the power to separate us from the Love of God that is in Christ Jesus our Lord." [1 John 2:5] "Whoever keeps His Word, truly in him the love of God is perfected. This is how we know we are in Him."

How can we know if we are included in God's Love? [1John 5:3] "for this is what Love for God is; to keep His commands. Now His commands are not a burden."

Did Christ give a new commandment while on earth or do away with the other commandments? [2John 5] "not as though I wrote a new commandment to you, but that which we have had from the beginning; that we love one another." Do you want a promise from Jesus Christ?]John 14:21] "The one who has My commands and keeps them is the one who loves Me. And the one who loves Me will be loved by My Father. I also will love him and reveal Myself to him." WHAT A PROMISE.! [John 14:24]" The one who doesn't love Me will not keep My words."

Jesus told the people while He walked among men on earth, "if you do not believe Moses who wrote about Me, you will not believe Me,John 5:24,42. [Rom 13:8-10] says that love for our neighbors and our Love to God is the fulfilling of God's Law. Paul is referring to the law of commandments written by God, given to Moses, meaning they cannot be changed. [Isa 40:8} "The Word of God stands forever." [Heb 13:8] "Jesus Christ is the same yesterday, today, and forever." We hear from the pulpits today that the Law of God was nailed to the cross, and no longer valid for Christians today. Do Christians believe what we hear today from the mouth of mortal man or should we believe the Word of God? We are told in [James 2:10] "Whoever shall keep the whole law, and yet stumble in one point, he is guilty of all." [James 4:17] "Therefore, to him who knows to do good and does not do it, to him it is sin."

Scripture reminds us that we can know if we know our Lord! [1 John 2:3] "Now by this we know that we know Him, if we keep His commandments." The best part of knowing our Lord is found in [1 John 4:18] "There is no fear in love, but perfect love cast out fear." make sure what you believe is Scripture! Nothing has changed sense Adam sinned. Jesus asked the Pharisees [Matt 15:3] "Why do you also transgress the commandments of God because of your tradition?" Will you or I be asked the same question by Christ? Jesus says in [Matt 15:8-9] "These people draw near to Me with their mouth, and honor Me with their lips, but their heart is far from Me, teaching as doctrine the commandments of men." A rich young ruler asked Jesus, [Matt 19:16-17] "What good thing shall I do to have eternal life?" Jesus replied, "Keep the commandments." Is there a record in Scripture where God has changed any one of His Laws of the commandments? Jesus spoke many times on the Sabbath and it was His custom to be in church on the Sabbath.

You may ask why so much about the Law of God, "His commandments." Honoring Christ and 'all' His commandments is not a popular thing to do in this sinful world, but it has never been. Even Peter denied Christ, but he repented. [Luke 21:33] "Heaven and earth will pass away, but My words will by no means pass away."

People today are no different than ages past, they want to be accepted by the world. [John 12:43] "for they loved the praise of men more than the praise of God." We all will be judged by God's Word, not by how we pleased the world. [John 12:48] "the word that I have spoken will judge him in the last day." Christ knows those who love Him! We know that the world will hate those who honor God by honoring His Law of Love. [2 Tim 3:12-15] "All who desire to live godly in Christ Jesus will suffer persecution." Christians need patience.

For thousands of years, Satan has palmed off falsehood for Truth. Those that united with Satan will see the total failure of his cause. Satan will in the end bow down and confess the justice of his sentence.

So again look at what is "Love".

God is Love.

Love cast out fear.

Love covers all sins.

Love is strong as death.

Nothing can separate us from the Love of God.

Nothing can separate us from the Love of Christ.

Love never fails.

Love suffers long and is kind.

He that loves God loves his brother also.

Owe no one anything except Love.

We purify our lives by loving one another.

If we love one another, God abides in us.

All the Law is fulfilled in one word—Love.

God proved His Love by giving His Son to die for our sins.

Those who love the Lord hate evil.

How can we abide in God's Love? Love is more than magic, and it will always will be, for Love still remains Life's mystery! There is nothing in life that love cannot change. love is unselfish, understanding and kind. Love sees with its heart and not with its mind. Love is the answer that everyone seeks and is the language that every heart speaks. Love cannot be bought, its priceless and free. It's a sweet mystery!

God's Love is like the rolling ocean, so deep and very wide. No force can ever hope to check or stop its surging tide. There is no measure for God's Love and yet we can have it all. Christ love is without parallel. The more we study His Divine character in the light of the cross, the more we see mercy, tenderness and forgiveness blended with justice, and we discern evidences of a love and tender pity surpassing a mother's sympathy for her wayward child.

Our need is heaven's forgiveness and peace and love in our soul. Money cannot buy it, intellect cannot procure it, wisdom cannot attain to it; you can never hope, by your own effort to secure it. But God offers it to man as a gift, without money or price. Don't wait to feel that you are forgiven, but say "I believe, it is so, not because I feel it, but because God has promised. There is a condition to this promise, that we pray according to the will of God. It is the will of God to cleanse us from sin.

Here is where many people fail; they do not believe that Jesus pardons them personally, individually. They do not take God at His word. God does not deal with us as men deal with one another. His thoughts are thought of mercy, love, and tender compassion. Christ says "Let the wicked forsake his ways, and the unrighteous man his thoughts; and let him return unto the Lord, and He will have mercy upon him." [Ezk 18:32 "I have no pleasure in the death of him that dies; wherefore turn your self, and live ye." With all these promises of the Bible, can you give doubt? Our lives will reveal whether God's Grace is dwelling within us. We will reflect Christ character in our lives. There is no genuine repentance, unless it works reformation in our life. Love will spring up in the heart of a Christian. The unconsecrated heart cannot produce Love. It is found only in the heart where Jesus reigns. He who is trying to become holy by his own works, is attempting an impossibility. It is the Grace of Christ alone, through faith that can make us holy.

Obedience is the service of Love. We do not earn salvation by our obedience; for salvation is the free gift of God, to be received by faith. But obedience is the fruit of faith and love. That so—called faith in Christ which professes to release men from the obligation of obedience to God, is not faith, but presumption. "By grace are ye saved through faith, but faith, if it hath not works, is dead." Jesus declared before He returned to heaven "I have kept My Father's commandments, and abide in His Love." John 15:10.

Jesus died for us, and now offers to take our sins and give us His righteousness. If you give yourself to Him as your Saviour, then, sinful as your life may have been, for His sake you are accounted righteous. Christ character stands in place of our character, and we are accepted before God just as if you had not sinned. The closer we come to Jesus the more faulty we will appear in our own eyes. The Love of Christ cannot dwell in the heart that does not realize its own sinfulness. When we become children of God, the Bible speaks of this as being born again. This is when we begin to grow, as the statute of men and women in Christ Jesus. Unless a person is "born from above" - John 3:3- he cannot become a partaker of the life which Christ came to give. Our growth as children of God depends upon our union with Christ. Christ bound Himself to humanity by a tie of Love that can never be broken by any power save the choice of man himself.

Our Savior's joy is the uplifting and redemption of fallen man. For this He counted not His life dear unto Himself, but endured the cross,despising the shame. This is the Love of Christ that cannot be overcome by anyone or anything in heaven or earth! This spirit of Christ self-sacrificing love is the spirit that pervades heaven. When this love for Christ is enshrined in man's heart, it cannot be hidden.

Love for Jesus will be manifested in a desire to work as Jesus worked, for the blessing and uplifting of others. The Bible was not written for the scholar alone; it was designed for the common people. The love of Christ, the Truths for salvation are made plain and clear as noon day, and none will mistake or lose their way except those who follow their own judgment instead of the plainly revealed truth of God. We should not take the testimony of any man as to what the Scriptures teach, but read and study for ourselves. Never should the Bible be studied without prayer. The word of God is not welcome to the proud, sin loving heart, and those unwilling to obey its requirements are ready to doubt its authority. To arrive at truth, we must have a sincere desire to know the truth and be willing to obey it.

[Ezk 33:11] "As I live—I have no pleasure in the death of the wicked; but that the wicked turn from his way and live! The Lord knows who loves Him, we cannot pretend to Him! The last prayer of Christ with His band of disciples gathered about Him, He said "Neither pray I for these alone, but for them also which believe in Me through their word-" John 17:20. The love of Christ cannot be understood, we have to accept His love by faith, and we reveal our love to Christ by the honor we have for His Law and the Love we have for Him and our fellow men.

Why would any person refuse the love of Christ in that He has done everything possible to save us. Oh, that man could accept Christ and His 'Law of Love' and not try to substitute the traditions of man for the commandments that reveal the Creator. Every week we are reminded; The Sabbath is a memorial of creation and every week we keep ever present the true reason why we worship, He is our Creator, and we are His creatures. Every Sabbath is to keep His truth before our minds, that God instituted the Sabbath in Eden, not on Mt Sinai as many believe today. The keeping of the Sabbath is a sign of loyalty to the true Creator God.

The Law of God, which Satan has reproached as the yoke of bondage, will be honored as the Law of liberty. the same spirit that prompted rebellion in heaven, still inspires rebellion on earth. Reproof of sin still arouses the spirit of hatred and resistance today. The Law of God is a law of Love and the foundation of the government of God, the happiness of all created beings depend upon their perfect accord with its great principles of righteousness. God takes no pleasure in a forced allegiance, and He grants freedom of will, that all may render Him voluntary service. Love cannot be forced! Love comes from a pure heart.

CHAPTER 16

DEATH!

WEBSTER'S DICTIONARY—"permanent ending of all life in a person" "state of being dead."

What causes death? [Ezk 18:4] "The person who sins is the one who will die!" [V-32] "For I have no pleasure in the death of one who dies." says the Lord God. Therefore turn and live!

We hear people today claim, that their loved ones are in heaven with Jesus. What does the Bible teach?

You can know without a doubt, for the truth is in God's Word. Many theories and doctrines popularly supposed to be derived from the Bible have no foundation in it's teaching, and indeed are contrary to the whole tenor of inspiration. Christians need to test their belief or doctrines with the Word of God to make sure it is correct. Many Christians are obvious to the fact that some of the belief system in modern Christian churches rely upon pagan tradition and beliefs, rather than the word of God. The idea that when people die, they either go to heaven or hell is not what Jesus said about His friend Lazarus who had died. [John 11:11-14] "These things said He and after that He said unto them, Our friend Lazarus sleepeth; but I go, that I may awake him out of sleep. Then said His disciples, Lord if he sleep, he shall do well, howbeit Jesus spake of his death, but they thought that He had spoken of taken of rest in sleep. Then Jesus said plainly, Lazarus is dead."

Jesus clearly demonstrated that the dead sleep. Had Lazarus gone to heaven, Jesus would have told His disciples that he was in heaven with the Father. After Lazarus was raised by Jesus, no one asked "What was it like in heaven? Tell us about heaven. No one needed to ask because it was common belief of that day that when someone died, they slept until the resurrection at the last day.

[Ps 146:4] "His breath goeth forth, he returneth to his earth; in that very day his thoughts perish." The scriptures also show that we will not rise again until Jesus returns. [Job 14:12] "So man lieth down, and riseth not; till the heavens be no more, they shall not awake, nor be raised out of their sleep."

Paul reinforced and clarified that this was his understanding-[1Thess 4:16] "For the Lord shall descend from heaven with a shout, with the voice of the archangel, and the trump of God; and the dead in Christ shall rise first." The misconception of many Christians today is that when they die they go directly to heaven, even though the day of judgment has not occurred yet. The Bible makes it clear that the dead cannot praise God, their thoughts have perished and they are asleep, [Ps115:17]-"The dead praise not the Lord, neither any that go down into silence."

Hell fire is an event and not a place. Bible writers believed that the wicked would be raised at the second resurrection, also known as the resurrection to damnation, which occurs 1000 years after the resurrection to life. Some believe that the wicked will burn forever and be tormented forever. We are told only those who are saved to the resurrection of life will live forever. The wicked will not live forever. Many have come to the conclusion that the wicked will be tormented forever and misunderstand; their punishment is forever, they will never live again. Sodom and Gomorrha are the example [Jude 7] of the fire that destroys sin. It is not burning today, it had eternal consequences. So will the fire at the end of this world. Its is a sad fact that today many Christians prefer to believe the doctored claims of those who proclaim God's Truth.

All who believe and love Christ will never die the death of Sin—"eternal death." When those who love Christ and live for Him die, they have assurance that when Christ comes to take those who love Him, they will hear His voice; just like those who heard His voice when He walked the earth before He died for our sins.

CHAPTER 17

WHY DID JESUS HAVE TO DIE?

Was there not another way to save man, His creation? [Rom 5:12] "Therefore, just as through one man, sin entered the world, and death through sin, and thus death spread to all men, because all sinned." "Rom 6:23"-"For the wages of sin is death, but the gift of God is eternal life in Christ Jesus our Lord."

Was there sin before a Law? Rom 5:13-15 "For until the law sin was in the world, but sin is not imputed when there is no law. never the less death reigned from Adam to Moses, even over those who had not sinned according to the likeness of the transgression of Adam, who is a type of him who was to come. But the free gift is not like the offense. For if by the one man's offense many died, much more the grace of God and the gift by the grace of the one Man, Jesus Christ abounded to many." [V-18] "Therefore as through one man's offense judgment came to all men, resulting in condemnation, even so through one Man's righteous act, the free gift came to all men, resulting in justification of life.

How does sin effect our life? [Rom 6:23] "The wages of sin is death. [James 4:17] "Therefore to him who knows to do good and does not do it, to him it is sin." [Rom 14:23] "for whatever is not from faith is sin."

Then how can mankind escape death? We must come to Christ, because He came to save sinners. {1Tim 1:15] "This is a faithful saying and worthy of all acceptance, that Christ came into the world to save sinners." [Gal 3:22] "but the Scriptures has confined all under sin, that the promise by faith in Jesus Christ might be given to those who believe." [Heb 5:9] "And having been perfected, He became the Author of eternal salvation to all who obey Him."

[Titus 3:5-6] "not by righteousness which we have done, but according to His mercy He saved us, through the washing of regeneration and renewing of the Spirit—whom He poured out on us abundantly through Jesus Christ our Savior."

[Acts 4:12] "Nor is there salvation in any other, for there is no other name under heaven given among men by which we must be saved,"

[1Cor 1:18] "For the message of the cross is foolishness to those who are perishing, but to us who are being saved, it is the power of God."

CHAPTER 18

THE MILLENNIUM AND THE SECOND DEATH.

When does the millennium take place? When does the millennium start and end? Where in Scripture can we find the answer's? What is the second death and who is involved? The book of Revelation is the book that most people haven't read or studied because they have been led to believe that they can't understand it, by preachers of the Gospel. But what does [Rev 1:3] say? "Blessed is he who reads and those that hear the words of this prophecy, and keep those things which are written in it, for the time is near." [V-7] "Behold He is coming with clouds, and every eye will see Him, even those that pierced Him."

This is when the angel of the Lord will bind Satan for a thousand years. What does Scripture say about what will be going on during the millennium?

Those that Christ saves will go with Christ to heaven as He has promised, those living and those who have been resting in the grave. [1Thess 4:16-17] "the Lord Himself shall descend from heaven with a shout, with the voice of the archangel, and with the trump of God: the dead in Christ shall rise first; Then we which are alive and remain shall be caught up together with them in the clouds, to meet the Lord: and so shall we ever be with the Lord."

[Rev 20:1-2] It is at this time when Satan will be bound with no one to tempt to sin, "breaking the Law of God." [Rev 20:6] "Blessed and Holy is he that hath part in the first resurrection; over such the second death hath no power, but they shall be priest of God and of Christ, and shall reign with Christ a thousand years." Scripture here says there is a first resurrection, then there must be a second resurrection! We know that only the righteous were raised when Christ comes, so the lost must still be in the graves! There has to be a second resurrection! When will this be? What happens to the living wicked when Christ comes? [Isa 26:21] "The Lord cometh out of His place to punish the inhabitants of the earth for their iniquity; the earth also shall disclose her blood, and shall no more cover her slain." Rev 19:17-18 "An angel standing in the sun, and He cried with a loud voice, saying to all the fowls that fly in the midst of heaven, come and gather yourselves together into the supper of the Great God; that ye may eat the flesh of kings, and the flesh of captains, and the flesh of mighty men, and the flesh of horses, and of them that sit on them—both small and great." All the living wicked will be destroyed at Christ coming. Satan then will have a thousand years without anyone to tempt and think about his choice he and the angels that chose to believe his lie. There is no place in Scripture that says Satan and his angels or that man kind will have a second chance to choose to obey God's Law.

At the end of the millennium "the rest of the dead—the wicked—will be resurrected, thus releasing Satan from the inactivity that had imprisoned him Rev 20:5,7. The rest of the dead —the wicked—lived not again until the thousand years were finished. This will be the first resurrection of the wicked who died before Christ came to take the righteous to heaven. This is the resurrection of Damnation. Why does Christ raise the wicked people to life only to end their existence again? the righteous were raised at His second coming, at the beginning of the millennium and have looked over the books of Christ to see for themselves that Christ was just in His judgment. Now the lost, themselves—including Satan and his angels—will confirm the justice of Christ's ways. [Rom 14:11-12] "As I live, saith the Lord, every knee shall bow to Me, and every tongue shall confess to God. This includes the saved with Christ and the lost people and Satan and his angels. [Rev 20:9] "Fire came down from God out of heaven and devoured them." {2 Peter 3:7] "But the heavens and the earth, which are now, by the same word are kept in store, reserved unto fire against the day of judgment and perdition of ungodly men." [2 Thess 1:-7-9] "in flaming fire taking vengeance on those who do not know God, and on those who do not obey the gospel of our Lord Jesus Christ. These shall be punished with everlasting destruction from the presence of the Lord and from the glory of His power." [Mal 4:1] "for behold, the day is coming, burning like an oven, And all the proud, yes, all who do wickedly will be stubble. And the day which is coming shall burn them up," Says the Lord of hosts, That will leave them neither root nor branch." {Rev 20:15] "Whosoever was not found written in the book of life was cast into the lake of fire." Also the devil and his angels and the false prophet and the beast are cast into the lake of fire Rev 20:10. [Rev 21:8] tells that this is the second death. According to Scripture, God promises eternal life only to the righteous. The wages of sin is death, not eternal life in hell fire.

Christ will end the power of death when He comes to set up His kingdom-Rom 6:23. {Heb 2:14] "that through His death-Jesus-will destroy him who had power of death, that is the devil." Christ says in [Matt 25:46] "that the wicked will suffer "everlasting punishment, not everlasting punishing." Rev 21:4 "There shall be no more death, neither sorrow, nor crying, neither shall there be any more pain."

Friend, if you love Jesus and want to spend eternity with Jesus and the righteous, and be free from temptations of "sin"-which is ignoring the Law of God. {Rev 22:14] "Blessed are they that do His commandments, that they may have right to the tree of Life, and may enter in through the gates into the City."

Everyone needs to read the last chapter of Revelation in God's Holy Bible, for in this chapter Christ tells what some of heaven will be like for His people to whom He takes to heaven. Please don't be deceived by what you hear someone teach or preach, read it for yourself as the Holy Spirit blesses you as you read and study for yourself.

CHAPTER 19

THE ORIGIN AND END OF EVIL

The origin of Evil or Sin has no explanation. Its impossible to explain the origin of sin as to a reason for it's existence. Scripture teaches that God was in no wise responsible for sin. Could excuse for sin be found or cause be shown, it would cease to be sin. The only definition of sin is that given in Scripture, the Word of God. It is "the transgression of the Law" 1 John 3:4. To excuse sin is to defend it. Sin is the outworking of a principle at war with God's great Law of Love, which is the foundation of the divine government for all of God's universe. God's law is for happiness of all created beings.

God desires from all His creatures the service of love. He takes no pleasure in a forced allegiance, and He grants freedom of will, that they render Him 'voluntary' service of love.

There was one who chose to pervert this freedom. Sin originated with him who, next to Christ chose to corrupt his wisdom by reason of his brightness to indulge a desire for self-exaltation. Lucifer being next to Christ allowed jealousy of Christ to prevail in his heart. Lucifer urged that the angels should obey the dictates of their own will.

Even the loyal angels could not fully discern Lucifer's character, or see to what his work was leading. Until fully developed, sin would not appear the evil thing it was. The angels could not discern the terrible consequences that would result from setting aside the divine law of God.

Infinite wisdom did not destroy Lucifer. The service of Love can alone be acceptable to God. Had God immediately blotted sin and Satan from existence, then the angels would have served God from fear, rather than from love. neither would the influence of the deceiver have been fully destroyed, nor would the spirit of rebellion been eradicated. Evil must be permitted to come to maturity, for the good of the entire universe through ceaseless ages. The justice and mercy of God and the immutability of His Law needed to be forever placed beyond all questions.

Satan's rebellion was to be a lesson to the universe through all coming ages. The working out of Satan's rule and the effects upon both men and angels would show what manner of fruit the setting aside the divine Law would have. It would testify that with the existence of God's government and His Law is bound up for the well being of all the creatures that He has made.

The same spirit that prompted rebellion in heaven, still inspires rebellion on earth today. Reproof of sin still arouses the spirit of hatred and resistance. When God's message of warning are brought home to the conscience, Satan leads men to justify themselves, and to seek others for sympathy in their course of sin. Instead of repenting, they excite indignation against the reprover, as if he were the cause of their difficulty. From the days of righteous Able to our own time, such is the spirit which is displayed toward those who dare to condemn sin. [Ex 34:6-7] "The Lord, the Lord God, merciful and gracious, long-suffering and abounding in goodness and truth, keeping mercy for thousands, forgiving iniquity and transgression and sin, and that will not by no means clear the guilty."

The mighty argument of the cross demonstrates to the whole universe that the course of sin which Lucifer had chosen was in no wise; chargeable upon the government of God. It is Satan that prompts the world to reject Christ. Satan exerts all his power to destroy the knowledge of our Savior's mercy and love.

Satan's true character was revealed at the cross. Satan had claimed that the transgression of God's law would bring liberty and exaltation; but it was seen to result in bondage and degradation. It was seen that Lucifer opened the door for the entrance of sin, by his desire for honor and supremacy.

The death of Christ was an argument in man's behalf that could not be over thrown. The penalty of the law fell upon Christ who was equal with God, and man was free to accept the righteousness of Christ. But it was not merely to accomplish the redemption of man that Christ came to earth to suffer and to die. Christ came to "magnify the Law and to make it honorable."

The inhabitants of this world now know how to regard God's Law. Christ died to demonstrate to all the worlds of the universe that God's Law is unchangeable. Could God's law been set aside, then the Son of God need not have yielded up His life to atone for our transgression. The death of Christ proves its immutable.

The cross of Calvary, while it declares the Law immutable, proclaims to the universe that the wages of sin is death.

The extermination of Lucifer and sin, in the beginning would have brought fear to angels and dishonor to God; will soon vindicate God's love and establish His honor before the universe of beings who delight to do His will, and in whose heart is His Law. The law of God which Satan has reproached as a yoke of bondage, will be honored as the Law of Liberty. The spirit which put Christ on the cross and death moves the wicked to destroy those who honor God's law. Those who are unwilling to accept the plain, cutting truths of the Bible, are continually seeking for pleasing fables that will quiet their conscience. Too wise in their own conceit to search the Scriptures with earnest prayer for divine guidance, they have no shield from delusion. Satan can present his counterfeit so closely resembling the truth that it deceives those who are willing to be deceived or demand to know the truth.

The last great conflict between truth and error is but the final struggle of the long standing controversy concerning the Law of

God. God's Holy Word which has been handed down to us at such a cost of suffering and blood, is but of little value to many. The Christian world has shown contempt for the Law of God, and the Lord will do just what He has declared that He would, He will withdraw His blessings from the earth, and remove His protecting care from those who are rebelling against His Law, and teaching and forcing others to do the same. Satan has control of all whom God does not guard.

The keeping of God's true Sabbath, in obedience to God's law, is evidence of loyalty to our Creator. In every generation God has sent His servants to rebuke sin, both in the world and in the church. But people desire smooth things spoken to them, and unvarnished truth is not acceptable. The popular ministry, like the Pharisees of old, will denounce the Truth a message of Satan, and stir up the sin-loving multitudes to revile and persecute those who proclaim the Bible Truth. [2Tim 3:12] "All that will live Godly in Christ Jesus shall suffer persecution," Men of God have suffered in past ages, Wycliffe—Huss—Luther—Tyndall—Wesley- all suffered and urged that all doctrines be brought to the test of the Bible. God's people dare not tamper with the word of God, dividing His Holy Law, calling one portion essential and another non-essential, to gain the favor and pleasure of the world.

Many forms of religion will be continued by people from whom the Spirit of God is withdrawn. God's Sabbath will become a controversy point through out all Christendom, and the religious and secular authorities will combine to enforce the observance of the first day of the week for worship. This same argument was brought against Christ, because Christ would not honor the way the leaders of the church wanted everyone to worship when Christ was on earth.

Will God forget those who honor His Law? Did God forget Joseph, Elijah or those men in the fiery furnace or Daniel in the lions den? The last great conflict between Truth and error is but the final struggle between the religion of the Bible and the religion of tradition. When one rejects the Truth in God's Word 'Holy

Bible' they are rejecting the Author of Scripture. [2 Peter 2:21] "For it would have been better for them not to have known the way of righteousness than, after knowing it, to turn back from the Holy commandment delivered to them."

Every person should study God's word that they will not be deceived by any religious person, church, or group of teachers. Read and study for yourself and know that Christ does not save by churches, groups, but He saves each person when He judges our hearts.

CHAPTER 20

TRUST NOT IN DECEPTION OF TRUTH IN GOD'S WORD!

Our Lord offers a better way to live. He offers us the opportunity to follow Him, to love Him, to worship Him and spare ourselves many of the problems we otherwise bring upon ourselves. Merely professing to follow the Lord is not what the Christian life is about.

Unlike many religions today, the religion of the Bible[both old and new Testaments] teach that salvation is by Grace alone. Nothing we do, can ever make us good enough to be accepted by God. Our good deeds however intended, however spirit-inspired, can never bridge the gap that sin has caused between God and humanity. If good works could save us, if good works could atone for Sin, if good works could pay our debt before God, then Jesus never would have had to die for us. Only the death of Jesus credited to us by faith, only the righteousness of Christ, which He wrought out in His life, which is then given to all who truly accept it, can save the sinner. SIN, is so contrary to the basic principles of Gods government, which is based on Love and free choice, that nothing less than the death of Christ could solve the problem created by sin.

What we say, do or think all maters, these thoughts and actions reveal the reality of our experience with God. Jesus only asks for our Love, and tells us how to express this Love by keeping His commandments. By our obedience to Christ is the only way we can express our love to Him.

Noah expressed his love for Christ when he obeyed and built the boat and was saved by Christ for his obedience. Noah didn't have to obey but he believed and trusted what God asked.

For by one man's offense [sin] many died, much more the Grace of God and the gift by the Grace of one Man, Jesus Christ abounded to many. By one man's disobedience many were made sinners, so also by one Man's obedience many will be made righteous. [Rom 11:56] "Grace does not come from works! Grace come's from God according to our faith. We show our faith in God by our obedience to God and His Law. [Heb 13:8-9] "Jesus Christ is the same yesterday, today and forever. Do not be carried away with various "doctrines". For it is good that the heart be established by Grace. [Jude 4} "For certain men have crept in unnoticed, who long ago were marked out for this condemnation, ungodly men, who turn the Grace of our God into lewdness and deny the only Lord God and our Lord Jesus Christ.

The only way that man can have a relationship with Christ is to love Him like Noah, Moses, Paul, and others.

1 John 4:8—He who does not love, does not know God, for God is Love.

1 John 5:3—For this is the Love of God, that we keep His commandments.

James 2:10—If we stumble on one of God's commandments, then we are guilty of all.

God help us all to love His Law of Love and be found faithful when He comes in the clouds of Glory!

TEN DEADLY TRAPS OF LUCIFER, THE DEVIL

Satan's Ten commandments:

1. You can be a Christian, Just don't invest any time in a relationship with Christ.
2. Don't bother to search or read the Bible, It doesn't apply today.
3. What you believe is unimportant.
4. Twist the words of the Bible to say what you want. Don't study too deeply, and prove your point by quoting only part of the verse.
5. God's Ten commandments were done away at the cross
6. Trust psychics,spirits, mediums and miracles.
7. You can believe that Jesus was a good man, just don't believe He was the Son of God in human form.
8. Don't be afraid of me, I am not a real individual.
9. The second coming of Christ is this, He is coming to each individual at death.
10. Jesus is coming again in secret Rapture.

CHAPTER 22

WHEN GOD WRITES!

We know that all Scripture is given by inspiration of God— [2 Tim 3:16]. Where in Scripture is there recorded that God Himself, wrote to us? Is there a record and why and when God wrote and when did this occur?

Scripture reveals that Christ was also God, and Jesus, the Word and Holy Spirit all inclusive- John1:1-4, 14; Colossians 1:16; Rev 4:11; Heb 11:3.

Christ talked to several people in the old Testament, like Adam and Eve; Cain; Noah; Abraham; Jacob; Moses and others while on earth before and after the cross. Others wrote what Jesus said.

When has Christ actually written and it has been recorded in Scripture? Scripture tells that God spoke to all Israel while they were at the base of Mt. Sinai. God spoke to Israel His law of Love, the commandments telling them to live by His law of Love.

God asked Moses to come up to Him on the mountain and He would give him tablets of stone which God wrote with His own fingers, the ten commandments, to teach them to the people of Israel.

The second time recorded of God writing is on the wall of the King Belshazzar's palace. The King saw part of the hand that wrote on the wall-Dan 5:5-12. this put so much fear in the King, that his knee's smote one another. Daniel was called to interpret the meaning of the writing on the wall-Dan 5:5-12. Daniel tells what is written," [MENE,MENE,TEKEL,UPHARSIN]" AND THE INTERPRETATION OF THE MEANING-'GOD HAS NUMBERED YOUR KINGDOM, AND FINISHED IT: YOU HAVE BEEN WEIGHED IN THE BALANCES, AND FOUND WANTING; YOUR KINGDOM HAS BEEN DIVIDED, AND GIVEN TO THE MEDES AND THE PERSIANS."

Belshazzar knew right from wrong, his father was Nebuchadnezzar who had been shone by God through dreams what was to take place in the world and Nebuchadnezzar didn't want to accept or believe and he revolted and made his own image to reflect what he wanted instead of what God said would take place in the future. [Dan 4:37] "tells that Nebuchadnezzar finally accepted God and served God. Belshazzar mocked what he knew of God and brought about the hand writing on the wall of the Palace.

The third time Christ wrote is recorded in [John 8:6-12] We are not told what Jesus wrote, but we know it brought conviction to the hearts of those that did see what Jesus wrote in the sand! We know that Christ does not condemn, He only wants everyone to come to repentance of their sin's and be saved-2 Peter 3:9.

The Scriptures was given and inspired by God to man. to record, that all may know He has provided salvation for all who choose and obey His laws.

The next promise of God writing is [Heb 8:10] "says the Lord, I will put My laws in their minds and write them on their hearts; and I will be their God, and they shall be My people." Again in [Jer 31:33] "I will put My laws into their hearts and in their minds I will write them." [Heb 8:10] "I will put My laws in their mind and write them on their hearts; and I will be their God, and they shall be My people."

Friend, will you acknowledge and allow Gods Law in your heart today so that very soon when Christ comes, He can write them on your heart and in your mind? [1 Peter 1:25] "But the word of the

Lord endures forever." Why not accept and trust in the Lord while there is time to worship Him? There is coming a day when all who ever lived on this earth will bow and worship, whose names have not been written in the Book of LIFE. At that time, it will be to late to ask forgiveness and to be saved [Rev 13:8}. Now is the time to acknowledge Christ and His Word and to Love Him. One day and very soon every person will see Christ coming in clouds to take those that love and acknowledge Him, by obeying His Law of Love. Only you and the Lord know your heart and mind. Have you surrendered to your Creator who created you and died for you and your sins? [Isa 49:16] "Tells that "I have inscribed you on the palms of My hands." Jesus does not force anyone to accept His Law of Love, its our choice. Will you allow Christ to write His Law of Love in your heart and in your mind? Christ has a claim upon every soul; but many choose a life of sin.

CHAPTER 23

"THE LORD'S DAY"

People today are so busy, they have very little time to read and study what's in God's Bible. Most people secretly wish that they could give God more of their time.

We should be very thankful that God understands the problems that face us today. God knew that as time passed and life became more complex, man would have a tendency to forget the relationship that existed between him and his Maker. therefore, God set aside a special time so man could refresh himself, setting aside his many problems, troubles and perplexities and renew his relationship with his Father.

The psychiatrist maintain's that if every person would put out of his mind all the daily perplexities for one day a week and relax completely, there would be little need for mental institutions.

God set aside such a day in which He wants us to renew our physical and spiritual strength. Learn about this day from Him. What does God call His special Day? [Rev 1:10] Its called the Lords Day. Which day did the Lord say He was Lord of? [Matt 12:8] "For the Son of Man is Lord of the Sabbath." [Isa 58:13] "a Holy day-honorable day-not doing your own ways-nor finding your own pleasures-nor speaking your own words." So we ask which day is the Sabbath or the Lord's Day? [Ex 20:8-11] "The seventh day is the Sabbath to the Lord your God.

When was this Sabbath created, blessed by God, and set aside as a Holy day by God? [Gen 2:1-4] At creation, the first week that God made everything and the seventh day was set aside as a Holy day for rest. God blessed the seventh day and declared it Holy, for He rested from all His work of creation.

In [John 1:1] we learn that it was Jesus who was the active agent of creation. It was Jesus therefore who rested on the Sabbath and blessed and sanctified it. For whom did God make the Sabbath? [Mark 2:27-28] "The Sabbath was made for man and not man for the Sabbath. therefore the Son of Man is Lord even of the Sabbath.

Some today claim that the Sabbath is Jewish and not for us today. There were no known Jews at creation week. The Jews were the heirs of Abraham. For the Lord says this in [Isa 56:1-7] "Happy is the man who does this, anyone who maintains this who keeps the Sabbath without desecrating it, and keeps his hand from doing evil——for the Lord says this; for the eunuchs who keeps My Sabbaths, and choose what pleases Me, and holds firmly to My covenant, I will give them, in My house and within My walls, a memorial and a name better than sons and daughters. I will give each of them an everlasting name that will never be cut off. /and the foreigners who convert to the Lord; ministers to Him, loves the Lord's name, and are His servants, all who keep the Sabbath without desecrating it, and hold firmly to My covenant——My house will be called a house of prayer for all nations.

"Cursed is the man who trust in mankind, who makes human flesh his strength and turns his heart from the Lord,"-Jer 17:5. the Lord predicted the fall of the Jewish nation if they failed to keep the Sabbath Holy-V-27.

Did Jesus leave us an example while He was on earth in regard to the Sabbath? What day did Jesus, while on earth honor as Sabbath? [Luke 4:16] "As usual, He entered the synagogue on the Sabbath Day. How did the followers of Christ honor the Sabbath after the crucifixion? [Luke 23:56] "they rested on the Sabbath according to the commandments."

After- [Saul]-Paul was converted and was preaching to the Jews, the Gentiles requested that Paul preach to them the next Sabbath. Had there been a change in the Sabbath then? [Acts 13:42-44] "they begged that these matters be presented to them the following Sabbath." There is no record of Paul preaching on a day other than the Sabbath-[Acts 17:2; Acts 18:3-4].

What day will God's people worship when in heaven and on the new earth? [Isa 66:22-23] "All mankind will come to worship Me, from one new moon to another, and from one Sabbath to another" says the Lord.

What does God ask His people to do in regard to His Holy Day? [Isa 58:13-14] "If you keep from desecrating the Sabbath, from doing whatever you want on My Holy Day; if you call the Sabbath a delight, and the Holy Day of the Lord honorable; if you honor it, not going your own ways, seeking your own pleasure, or talking too much, then you will delight yourself in the Lord, and I will make you ride over the heights of the land, and let you enjoy the heritage of your father Jacob." 'For the mouth of the Lord has spoken.'

How can we express our love to God for creating and redeeming us? [1 John 5:1-3] "By this we know that we love the children of God, when we love God and keep His commandments. For this is the Love of God that we keep His commandments. And His commandments are not burdensome." Whom should the Christian follow in choosing a day of worship?

Many times in Scripture, God states that the one act that sets Him apart as the true God, is His creative power. It was God who created the world. this earth did not come into existence by some strange chance, bang or explosion, or evolutionary process. The Sabbath was made as the memorial of His creative ability. This relationship of creature to Creator is the true basis for all worship. Since this relationship can never be changed, through all eternity, all creation will worship God on "His Sabbath Day."

Think of Eve and Adam in the garden and the choices they made, and about their son Cain and the choice he made. What about the nation Israel, the Pharisees and Sadducees, they thought they knew better, also Saul before the Lord spoke to him and he was converted. To be more personal, what about Christians today and the day we have chosen to worship? Are we doing what God has asked and really, some have been taught that the Sabbath was changed. Some believe because Christ rose from the grave on the first day of the week, this should be kept as the sabbath. Some admit they do not know why a change was made from the seventh day as God had made, to Sunday the first day. Some say they keep Sunday because their families had kept it for ages and they were merely following tradition. Some say, because Christ rose from the tomb!

There is only one safe guide to follow in this world of religious confusion. There is only one rule of right the "HOLY BIBLE" It will always be safe to build your faith on Bible facts. Jesus kept the Sabbath when He was on earth. We cannot safely follow our feelings, for God has told us, "There is a way that seems right to a man, But its end is the way of death." Proverbs 16:25.

Everyone has a right to make their own choice in the matter of a day of worship, but they do not have the right to choose their "consequences". Don't look for a church to lead you to truth. Let the TRUTH lead you to a church that is worshiping as God has asked in His Word.

CHAPTER 24

THE DAY OF THE LORD?

We hear today many say they worship on the Lord's Day or the Day of the Lord. As a child, my family had not known any other day that anyone worshiped on. All my life, I have studied the Bible for information about the Lord's day or the day of the Lord. I have read the Bible through and through several times and never connected the first day of the week as the Lord's Day to worship.

The Lord's Day is referred to in [Rev 1:10], "I was in the spirit on the Lord's day, and heard behind me a great voice, as of a trumpet."

Looking in the Old Testament for text's about the Lord's Day and the Day of the Lord, are several, but nothing about a day to worship our Lord on! {Isa 2:12] "For the day of the Lord of hosts shall be upon every one that is proud and lofty, and upon every one that is lifted up; and shall be brought low." [Isa 12:6] "For the day of the Lord is at hand; it shall come as a destruction from the Almighty." [Isa 13:6] "Howl ye; for the day of the Lord is at hand; it shall come as a destruction from the Almighty." [Isa 13:9] "Behold, the day of the Lord cometh, cruel both with wrath and fierce anger, to lay the land desolate; and He shall destroy the sinners thereof out of it." [V-10] "For the stars of heaven and the constellations thereof shall not give their light; the sun shall be darkened in his going forth, and the moon shall not cause her light to shine." [Joel 1:15] "Alas for the day! For the day of the Lord is at hand, and as a destruction from the Almighty shall it come." [Joel 2:1] "Let all the inhabitants of the land tremble; for the day of the Lord cometh, for it is nigh at hand." [V-11] "for the day of the Lord is great and very terrible; and who can abide it." [Joel 3:14] "Multitudes, multitudes in the valley of decision; for the day of the Lord is near in the valley of decision." [V-15] "The sun and the moon shall be darkened, and the stars shall withdraw their shining." [Amos 5:18] "Woe to you who desire the Day of the Lord! To what end is it for you? The Day of the Lord is darkness, and not light." [Amos 8:11-12] "Behold the days come, saith the Lord God, that I will send a famine in the land, not a famine of bread, nor a thirst for water, but of hearing the words of the Lord. And they shall wonder from sea to sea, and from north even to the east, they shall run to and fro to seek the word of the Lord, and shall not find it." [Obadiah 15] "For the day of the Lord is near upon all the heathen; as thy hast done, it shall be done unto thee; thy reward shall return upon thine own head." [Zeph 1:7] "Hold thy peace at the presence of the Lord; for the day of the Lord is at hand. [V-14] "the great day of the Lord is near, it is near, and casteth greatly, even the voice of the day of the Lord; the mighty man shall cry there bitterly." [V-15] "That day is a day of wrath, a day of trouble and distress, a day of wasteness and destruction, a day of darkness and gloominess, a day of clouds and thick darkness." [Zech 14:1] "Behold, the day of the Lord cometh, and thy spoil shall be divided in the midst of thee." All these text point to the coming of our Lord, not a day of worship or a Sabbath.

What does the New Testament say about the Day of the Lord, and worshiping for Christians? [Mark 2:28] "Therefore the Son of Man is also Lord of the Sabbath. [Acts 2:20] "The sun shall be turned into darkness, and the moon into blood before that great and notable day of the Lord." [1Cor 5:5] "To deliver such an one unto Satan for the destruction of the flesh, that the spirit may be saved in the day of the Lord." [1 Thess 5:2] "For yourselves know perfectly that the day of the Lord so cometh as a thief in the night." [V-4]

"But ye, brethren are not in darkness, that the day should overtake you as a thief." [2Peter3:10] "but the day of the Lord will come as a thief in the night; in the which the heavens shall pass away with a great noise, and the elements shall melt fervent heat, and the earth also and the works that are therein shall be burned up." [Matt 12:8] "For the Son of Man is Lord even of the Sabbath." [Mark 2:28] "The Son of Man is also Lord of the Sabbath."

When we read for ourselves that the world has adopted a day for the Sabbath of their own, we will be convinced that the world has done just what Cain did [Gen 4:2-11] had done. Cain chose what he wanted to offer to the Lord, instead of what the Lord asked. Mankind has done the same for the Day of worship. We have a warning from God in [Jude 11] "Woe to them! For they have gone in the way of Cain, have run greedily in the way of Balaam for profit, and perished in rebellion of Korah."

What is the choice that you and I have made, God's way or the way of Cain? No one knows if we will be here tomorrow, make your choice today. God wants to save every person on this earth, but, it's our choice. God is all about Love! We love Him or we deny Him! God will not force anything upon anyone who does not understand Love! He loves us to much!

People who love the Lord and are looking for His soon return, need to know what our Lord has revealed in His word, not believing what the world has accepted. We can read what happened to the world before the flood came, what people accepted as truth then. Truth is not popular in the world then or even now!

Jesus said [Matt 7:15] "Beware of false prophets." [V-21] "Not everyone who says to Me, Lord, Lord, shall enter the kingdom of heaven." [V-22] "Many will say to Me in that day, Lord-Lord, have we not prophesied in Your Name, and done many wonders in your name?" [V-23] "And then I will declare to them, I never knew you; depart from Me, you who practice lawlessness." Does the world honor God's Law of commandments or parts that fits their life-style?

The world has taken prayer out of schools, and our government, and the Bible from government buildings. Some people would have all who honor God's Law done away with and have tried to do just that in our history, but God has provided that His Truth will prevail and the just will live by His Law for eternity to come.

Have you read what Scripture says about those that go to heaven with Christ when He comes? [Isa 66:23] "And it shall come to pass, that from one new moon to another, and from one Sabbath to another, shall all flesh come to worship before Me, saith the Lord."

What is your decision about the Lord's Day, a day of wrath or worship? Scripture makes very plain the day of worship that God created for mankind to worship our Creator God. Which will you and I choose? I pray we will choose the day God created for worship to our Creator God.

CHAPTER 25

FAITH AND THE LAW

Blessings come from God on the basis of faith, not Law! The Law of God declares men guilty and imprisons them; Faith sets men free to enjoy liberty in Christ. But liberty is not license. Freedom in Christ means freedom to produce the fruits of righteousness through a Spirit-led lifestyle.

Christ has freed the Christian believer from bondage to the Law (legalism) and a license to sin and placed him in a position of liberty. The transforming Cross provides for the believer's deliverance from the curse of sin, law, and self. The Apostle Paul shows that the believer is no longer under the curse of the Law but is saved by faith alone. Had not Jesus came, all mankind would die with no hope for salvation and life with our Lord.

When Christ gave His life on the cross, no longer did we need to offer a lamb, [which pointed to when Jesus was to be our Lamb]. Man is saved by Faith alone. God raised up the disciples and Paul to deliver man from the bondage of the sacrifices of lambs.

The impact of the Truth concerning the laws of Scripture is staggering; how men has confused the Law of sacrifice of lambs, pointing to the Lamb of God and God's law of commandments which God gave to Moses, which were a copy of the law in heaven. [Gods Law of commandments was not nailed to the cross as some teach today.] The Law of sacrifices was nailed to the cross, the [Lamb of God] not a lamb of man. The sacrifice of lambs by man, pointed to the day when Christ was our Lamb. This Lamb of God "Jesus" is our hope and salvation! No longer does mankind need to sacrifice a lamb, because Jesus Christ is our Lamb when we accept and choose to honor His Law. We may profess what we will, but unless our life corresponds with our profession, our faith is dead. Words and acts testify plainly what is in the heart. All need to remember Simon Peter, how he thought his faith was strong. and the warning given Jesus gave Peter. Luke 22:31 "Simon, behold, Satan hath desired to have you, that he may sift you as wheat." Peter's self-confidence proved his ruin. When Christ needed Peter most, Peter stood on the side of Satan, and denied his Lord. Many today stand where Peter stood when in self-confidence they could fall easy prey to Satan's devices by not knowing the Scriptures.

CHAPTER 26

THE LAW AND THE GOSPEL

What can bring the sinner to the knowledge of his sins unless he knows what sin is? The only definition of sin is in the Word of God, given in [1 John 3:4] "Sin is the transgression of the Law." The gospel without the Law is inefficient and powerless. The law and the gospel are a perfect whole.

The Law and the Gospel, both have a place in God's Plan to save man. The Law of the Ten commandments sets forth the standard of righteousness and consequently makes sin known. [Isaiah 51:7] "Harken unto Me, ye that know righteousness, the people in whose heart is My Law." Why do they know righteousness? It is because God's Law is in their heart and His law is the standard of righteousness. [Rom 3:20] states "by the Law is the knowledge of sin." [Romans 7:7] "What shall we say then? Is the Law sin? God forbid. Nay, I had not known sin, but by the Law; for I had not known lust, except the law had said, Thou shalt not covet."

The Law of God is founded upon Love and teaches us how to express our love both to God and to man. "Therefore Love is the fulfilling of the Law." You see, the law reveals the sin from which it is unable to save us, and in that way urges us to Christ as the One who can supply the righteousness required, as it is written in [Rom 10:4] "For Christ is the end of the Law for righteousness to every one that believes." Our obedience to God's Law, is not to be saved, but because we are saved. It is not our doing, but His doing. [Galations 5:6] all true obedience is the obedience of Love. "Love is the fulfilling of the law."—Rom 13:10.

Will failing to keep the Sabbath day holy really be regarded by God as a bad thing? The Sabbath commandment is no more important than the rest of the Ten commandments, it is no less important either! When a person breaks one of the commandments —whichever one it is—God regards that as being just as serious as breaking the rest of them. [James 2:10] "Whoever shall keep the whole Law, yet stumble in one point, he is guilty of all." Why is this so important that we keep God's Sabbath? God explains this {John 14:15] "If you love Me, keep My commandments."

The Sabbath was given to all mankind to commemorate the work of Creation. As the tree of Life was placed in the midst of the garden of Eden, so the Sabbath command is placed in the midst of the Law of God. As the tree was the test of Adam's obedience, so the fourth commandment is the test that God has given to prove the loyalty of all His people.

Halfhearted Christians are worse than infidels; for their deceptive words and noncommittal position lead many astray. The infidel shows his colors. The lukewarm Christian deceives both parties. He is neither a good worldling nor a good Christian. Satan uses him to do a work no one else can do. Thank our Lord, there is still time for them to repent. Christians need to guard against dishonoring God by professing to be His people, and then going directly contrary to His will.

The Sabbath question is a vital one for the whole world. If we give up the Sabbath, soon the church goes; and if we give up the Church, the home goes, and as the home goes, the nation goes. And sad to say, that is the direction which millions of people are traveling today.

In this world, the Sabbath has been a perpetual reminder of creation and of recreation, or redemption. We read in {Isa 66:23] that

Sabbath keeping will continue beyond the end of this present world? "And it shall come to pass that from one new moon to another, and from one Sabbath to another, shall all flesh come to worship before Me, saith the Lord."

CHAPTER 27

GOD'S EARTHLY STOREHOUSE TO SUPPORT HIS CHURCH

What claim does God have for supporting His Church? [Ps 24:1] "The earth is the Lord's, and the fulness thereof; the world and they that dwell therein." In Haggai 2:8 He declares that the silver and the gold are His. In Psalm 79:13 He says that we are His people, the sheep of His pasture. How can God claim ownership? [Genesis 1:1] "He made the sea; it is His, So is the earth." [Ps 95:5] "—God created man; therefore, we are His. "Know ye that the Lord He is God: it is He that hath made us, and not we ourselves Psalm 100:3.

Acts 17:28—"In Him we live, and move, and have our being." Christ redeemed us after we were lost because we sinned. We all belong to Him, yet Christ has left the choice to us!

Deut 8:18—"And you shall remember the Lord your God, for it is He who gives you power to get wealth."

So friend we are twice His—God made us, and He bought us with His blood at the cross of Calvary.

When everything belongs to God, how are we to relate to these possessions of God? Give back to God your entrusted possessions, and more will be entrusted to you. keep your possessions to your self, and you will lose the reward of the life to come. What God blesses is blessed. Ps 37:16 "a little that a righteous man hath is better than the riches of many wicked." Pros 3:9-10 "Honor the Lord with thy substance, and with the first fruits of all thine increase; so shall thy barns be filled with plenty, and thy presses shall burst out with new wine."

A story of a little boy and his example of his knowledge of the ownership of all things, helps us understand that the source and Creator of all, wants to bless those who acknowledge the ownership of all things,

"A little boy named William was 16 years old and poor, just starting out to make his way in life. He knelt on a tow path with the captain of a canal boat and listened to the captain's prayer. The captain said to the youth, "Someday, someone will be the leading soap-maker in New York. It might as well be you. You know soap-making and candle-making. Make an honest soap, and give a full pound. Make an honest soap and give the Lord what belongs to Him. That boy was William Colgate. He did pay his tithe—first, one tenth, then two tenths; later three, four, and five tenths. Finally he gave it all. Jesus says [Luke 6:38] "Give and it shall be given unto you."

CHAPTER 28

WISDOM; DO YOU WANT TO BE WISE?

Prov 1:5-A wise man will hear and increase learning and will attain counsel.

V-7—The fear of the Lord is the beginning of knowledge, but fools despise wisdom.

V-10—if sinners entice you, do not consent.

Prov 2:3—let not mercy and truth forsake you—Write them on the tablets of your heart.

V-5-6—Trust in the Lord—lean not on your understanding.

Prov 3:35—The wise shall inherit glory, but shame shall be the legacy of fools.

Prov 5:21—The ways of man are before the eyes of the Lord, and He ponders all his paths.

Prov 6:23—The commandment is a lamp, and the Law is a light.

Prov 7:2—Keep My commands and live, and My Law as the apple of your eye.

Prov 8:13—The fear of the Lord is to hate evil. Pride and arrogance and the evil way.

V:35—Whoever finds Me finds life and obtains favor from the Lord.

Prov 9:10—The fear of the Lord is the beginning of wisdom,knowledge of the Holy One is understanding.

Peov 10:1—A wise son makes a glad father, but a foolish son is grief of his mother.

V-12—Hatred stirs up strife, but love covers all sins.

V-18—Whoever hides hatred has lying lips.

V-19—He who restrains his lips is wise.

V-27—The fear of the Lord prolongs days, but the wicked will be shortened.

Prov 11:7—When a wicked man dies, his exceptions will perish.

V-14—Where there is no council, the people fall.

V-18—he who sows righteousness will have a sure reward.

V-25—the generous soul will be rich.

V-28—He who trust in his riches will fall, but the righteous will flourish like foliage.

Prov 12:1-whoever loves instruction loves knowledge,but he who hates correction is stupid.

V-15—The way of a fool is right in his own eyes, but he who heeds counsel is wise.

V-17—He who speaks truth declares righteousness, but a false witness, deceit.

V-19—The truthful lip shall be established forever.

V-22-Lying lips are an abomination to the Lord, but those who deal truthful are His delight.

Prov 13:3—He who guards his mouth preserves his life.

v-10- By pride comes nothing but strife.

V-13-He who despises the Word will be destroyed, but he who fears the commandment will be rewarded.

V-14—The law of the wise is a fountain of life, to turn one away from the snares of death.

V-18—He who regards a rebuke will be honored.

V-21—Evil pursues sinners, but to the righteous, good shall be repaid.

V-22—a good man leaves an inheritance to his children's children.

V-24—He who spares his rod hates his son, but he who loves him disciplines him promptly.

Prov 14:3—In the mouth of a fool is a rod of pride.

V-12—There is a way that seems right to a man, but its end is the way of death.

V-22—Mercy and Truth belong to those who devise good.

V-26—In the fear of the Lord there is strong confidence.

Prov 15:1-A soft answer turns away wrath, but a harsh word stirs up anger.

V-7—The lips of the wise disperse knowledge, but the heart of the fool does not do so.

V-12—A scoffer does not love one who corrects him, nor will he go to the wise.

V-16—Better is a little with the fear of the Lord, than great treasure with trouble.

V-31—The ear that hears the rebukes of life will abide among the wise.

Prov 16:2-all the ways of man are pure in his own eyes, but the Lord weighs the spirits.

V-5—Everyone proud in heart is an abomination to the Lord.

V-25—There is a way that seems right to a man, but its end is the way of death.

v-32-He who is slow to anger is better than the mighty, he who rules his spirit than he who takes a city.

Prov 17:1—Better is a dry morsel with quietness, than a house full of feasting with strife.

V-9-He who covers a transgression seeks love, but he who repeats a matter separates friends.

V-10—Rebuke is more effective for a wise man than a hundred blows on a fool.

V-11—An evil man seeks only rebellion.

V-17—A friend loves at all times.

V-22-a merry heart does good like medicine, but a broken spirit dries the bones.

V-27-he who has knowledge spares his words, and a man of understanding is of a calm spirit.

Prov 18:10-The name of the Lord is a strong tower; The righteous run to it and are safe.

V-15-The heart of the prudent acquires knowledge, and the ear of the wise seeks knowledge.

Prov 19:5—A false witness will not go unpunished.

V-14—A prudent wife is from the Lord.

V-16-He who keeps the commandments keeps his soul, but he who is careless of his ways will die.

V-23—The fear of the Lord leads to life.

Prov 20:1-Wine is a mocker, strong drink is a brawler, who ever is led by it is not wise.

V-3—any fool can start a quarrel.

V-4—a lazy man will not plow because of winter, he will beg during harvest and have nothing.

V-11-Even a child is known by his deeds.

V-28—Mercy and Truth preserve the King.

Prov 21:13-Whoever shuts his ear to the cry of the poor will also cry himself and not be heard.

V-17-he who loves pleasure will be a poor man, he who loves wine and oil will not be rich.

V-23—whoever guards his mouth and tongue keeps his soul from trouble.

Prov 22:1—a good name is to be chosen rather than great riches.

V-4—by humility and fear of the Lord are riches and honor and life.

V-6-Train up a child in the way he should go and when he is old he will not depart from it.

v-15-foolishness is bound up in the heart of a child, the rod of correction will drive it far from him.

Prov 25:5-riches certainly make themselves wings; they fly away like an eagle toward heaven.

V-9—do not speak in the hearing of a fool, for he will despise the wisdom of your words.

V-17—Do not envy sinners, but be zealous for the fear of the Lord all the day.

V-23—buy the Truth and do not sell it, also wisdom and instruction and understanding.

Prov 24:9-the divising of foolishness is a sin and the scoffer is an abomination to men.

Prov 25:11-A word fitly spoken is like apples of gold in settings of silver.

Prov 26:4—Do not answer a fool according to his folly.

Prov 26:12—Do you see a man wise in his own eyes? There is more hope for a fool than for him.

V-20—Where there is no tale bearer, strife ceases.

Prov 27:5—Open rebuke is better than love carefully concealed.

Prov 28:1—The wicked flee when no one pursues, but the righteous are bold as a lion.

V-4—Those who forsake the Law praise the wicked, but such keep the Law contend with them.

V-7—Who ever keeps the law is a discerning son.

V-9—One who turns away his ear from hearing the Law, even his prayers is an abomination.

V-13—He who covers his sins will not prosper, but whoever confesses and forsakes them will have mercy.

V-23-He who rebukes a man will find more favor afterward than he who flatters with the tongue.

v-27—He who gives to the poor will not lack.

Prov 29:5—He who flatters his neighbor spreads a net for his feet.

V-11-A fool vents all his feelings, but a wise man holds the back.

V-15—The rod and rebuke give wisdom, but a child left to himself brings sham to his mother.

V-17- Correct your son and he will give you rest—he will give delight to your soul.

V-18—Happy is he who keeps the Law.

V-23—A man's pride will bring him low.

V-25—The fear of man brings a snare, but whoever trusts in the Lord shall be safe.

Prov 30:5—Every word of God is pure, He is a shield to those who put their trust in Him.

V-6—Do not add to His Words, lest He rebuke you and you be found a liar.

Prov 31:10—Who can find a virtuous wife? For her worth is far above rubies.

V-30—Charm is deceitful and beauty is passing. But a woman who fears the Lord, she shall be praised.

CHAPTER 29

CHRIST SOON COMING— WHEN WILL IT BE?

There is a day that God has appointed for the close of this world's history. When is this? We are told in [Matt 24:14] "This gospel of the Kingdom shall be preached in all the world for a witness unto all nations; and then shall the end come." This doctrine of the second advent is the very key note of Sacred Scripture. Holy men of old looked forward to the advent of the Messiah in glory, as the consummation of their hope. this solemn fact is to be kept not only before the people of the world, but before our own churches also.

Christ has given signs of His coming. He declares that we may know when He is near, even at the door. the nations are in unrest. False prophets will arise and deceive many-Matt 24:11. Gluttony and intemperance and great moral depravity in the world. Eating and drinking and dressing for the world. The Land is filled with violence, war, murder in every land. Ships will be hurled into the depths of the sea. Fires will break out unexpectedly and no human effort will be able to quench them. Disasters by rail will become more and more frequent. Death without a moments warning will occur on the great lines of travel. The waters of the deep will overflow their boundaries. Property and life will be destroyed by fire and flood. Earthquakes will take place when least expected.

The reports of fraudulent transactions, murders, and crimes of every kind are coming to us daily. Iniquity is so common a thing that it no longer shocks the senses as it once did.

God has a purpose in permitting these calamities to occur. they are one of His means of calling men and women to their senses.

No one knows the definite time for the coming of our Lord. For forty years the unbelief, murmuring, and rebellion shut out ancient Israel from the land of Canaan. The same sins have delayed the entrance of modern Israel into the heavenly Canaan. It is the unbelief, the worldliness, unconsecrated, and strife among the Lord's professed people that have kept us in this world of sin and sorrow so many years.

We know that among God's church, there are defective members, that there are tares amid the wheat. There are evils existing in the church, and will be until the end of the world, the church is to be the light of the world, even though polluted by sin. Jesus will have His angels separate the wheat and the tares.

The doctrine of the second advent has been neglected in our churches. Christ foretold the backsliding that would exist just prior to His second advent. there would be, as in the days of Noah the stir of worldly business and pleasure, buying, selling, planting, building, marrying, and given in marriage—forgetfulness of God and the future life. Christ has foretold the condition of the church at this time-[Rev 3:1,3] "Thou hast a name that thou livest, and are dead. if therefore thou shalt not watch, I will come on thee as a thief, and then shalt not know what hour I will come upon thee."

It was not the scholarly theologians who had an understanding the Truth about Christ "first coming". Had they been faithful watchmen, diligently and prayerfully searching the Scriptures, they would have known the time for Christ coming was nigh. The prophecies would have opened to them what was about to take place. Their ignorance was the result of sinful neglect.

What a lesson is this wonderful story of Bethlehem! How it rebukes our unbelief, our pride and self—sufficiency. How it warns us to beware, lest by our indifference we also fail to discern the signs of the times.

No person is safe for a day or an hour without prayer. Unless we become vitally connected with God, we can never resist the effects of self-love, self-indulgence, and temptation to sin. When worldiness is allowed to come in, we have no desire to pray, no desire to commune with God, who is the source of strength and wisdom, His Spirit will not abide in us.

Our profession of faith is not our guarantee in that day, but the state of our affections. We are placed on trial in this world, to determine our fitness for future life. those who are watching and waiting for the appearing of Christ in the clouds of heaven will not be mingling with the world in pleasure societies and gatherings merely for their own amusement. If we can take Jesus with us and maintain a prayerful spirit we are perfectly safe.

The cities of today are fast becoming like Sodom and Gomorrah. God is withdrawing His Spirit from the wicked cities. The wicked are being bound up in bundles, bound up in trusts, and unions.

Political corruption is destroying love of justice and regard for Truth, even in free America rulers and legislators, in order to secure public favor, will yield to the popular demand for a law enforcing Sunday observance. This substitution of the false for the True is the last act in the drama of worship. When the laws of men are exalted above the Law of God, we know that the time has come for God to work. This substitution of Sunday in place of the Bible Sabbath, is the last act in the drama on this earth. When this becomes universal God will reveal Himself.

God has His people in all the churches. the greater part of God's people are in the various churches professing the protestant faith. God will raise up from among the common people men and women to do the work, even as old, He called fishermen to be His disciples. God will raise up and exalt among us those who are taught by the unction of His Spirit rather than by the outward training of scientific institutions. The ordinary mind, trained to obey the "Thus saith the Lord" is better qualified for God's work than are those who have capabilities but do not employ them rightly.

The poor man is Christ's witness. He cannot appeal to histories or so called science, but gather from the Word of God powerful evidence and Truth. When divine power is combined with human effort, the work will spread like fire in the stubble. Every truly honest person will come to the light of Truth. Family connections, church relations, will be powerless to stay them now.

There will only be two classes in the world in the end time. Each will either have the Seal of God, or the Mark of the Beast or his image. Everyone will have sufficient knowledge to make his decision. [Ezk 20:12] God declares-"I gave them My Sabbath, to be a sign between Me and them, that they might know that I am the Lord that sanctify them."

Church members who have received the light of the Truth and been convicted, but trusted the salvation of their soul to the ministers, will learn in the day of God that no soul can pay the ransom for their transgressions. God's Word is made of none effect by false shepherds.

Though no man knoweth the day or the hour of Christ coming, we are instructed and required to know when it is near. We are further taught that to disregard His warning, and refuse or neglect to know when His advent is near, will be as fatal for us as it was for those who lived in the days of Noah. [Rev 3:3] "if therefore thou shall not watch, I will come on thee as a thief, and thou shalt not know what hour I will come upon thee." But some bold scoffers and even by some professed ministers of Christ will not know.

The time in which we live today is likened unto the Bible story of the ten virgins. They (all) slumbered and slept. There is two classes represented here. All had lamps— "Bibles"—but the foolish took no oil with them. The foolish ones depended upon the faith of their brethren, without understanding the truth or the genuine work of Grace in the heart. Those whose faith was based on a personal knowledge of the Bible had a rock beneath their feet.

Satan will try to impersonate the coming of our Lord, but don't be confused. Scripture is very clear about how Christ will come! We may hear that Christ has come in a distant area or country, and there will be those who will go to see him. When Jesus Christ comes, it will be no secret! Jesus Christ will not come alone, by Himself. [Jude 14-15] "Behold, the Lord cometh with ten thousand of His saints, to execute judgment upon all, and to convince all that are ungodly among them of all their ungodly deeds."[Rev 1:7] "Every eye shall see Him, even those who pierced Him."

A message was sent from heaven to the world in Noah's day, and their salvation depended upon the manner in which they treated that message. As they rejected the message then, people today reject the teachings of Scripture, God withdraws His Spirit and leaves them to the deceptions which they love. For seven days the people; just before the rain started to fall, knowing their doom was fixed, continued their careless pleasure—loving life, and mocking the warnings of impending judgment. "So says our Saviour, shall also the coming of the Son of Man be" Matt 24:39.

CHAPTER 30

WHAT DOES GOD'S HOLY WORD SAY ABOUT CHRIST COMING?

Ps 50:3,5—Our God shall come and shall not keep silent.—Gather My saints together to Me.

Isa 2:17-21—The Lord alone will be exalted in that day—They shall go into the holes of the rocks and into the caves of the earth—when He arises to shake the earth mightily.—Go into the clefts of the rocks, —-.

Isa 35:4-6—Behold your God will come with vengeance. With the recompense of God. He will come and save you. Then the eyes of the blind shall be opened, and the ears of the deaf shall be unstopped. The lame shall leap like a deer, and the tongue of the dumb sing.

Isa 66:15-For the Lord will come with fire, And with His chariots,

Dan 2:34-35—The Lords coming is likened to a stone cut without hand and smote the earth and all the kingdoms. V-44-45 God's Kingdom that will never be destroyed.

Matt 24:27 "for as the lighting comes from the East and flashes to the West, so also will the coming of the Son of Man be."

V-30—then the sign of the Son of Man will appear in the heaven, and all the tribe of the earth will morn, and they will see the Son of Man coming on the clouds of heaven with power and great glory.

V-31—He will send His angels with a great sound of a trumpet, and they will gather together His elect from the four winds, from one end of heaven to the other.

V-36-44—but the day and the hour no man knows, not even the angels of heaven, but My Father only. —But as the days of Noah were, so also will the coming of the Son of Man be. —Therefore you be ready, for the Son of man is coming at an hour you do not expect.

Matt 25:—When the Son of Man comes in His glory, and all the holy angels with Him, then He will sit on the throne of His glory.

Matt 26:64—hereafter, you will see the Son of Man sitting at the right hand of the power, and coming on the clouds of heaven.

Mark 13:5-37—Take heed that no one deceives you. For many will come in My name and deceive many.—The Gospel must first be preached to all the nations. [V-21-22] If anyone says to you, Look, here is Christ! or Look, he is there! Do not believe it. For false christ and false prophets will rise and shows signs and wonders to deceive, if possible, even the elect.—[V-32] —but the day and the hour no one knows, not even the angels in heaven, nor the Son, but only the Father. [V-37] I say to all, 'Watch'.

Luke 17:23-24—And they will say unto you, "Look here!" or Look there, Do not go after them or follow them. For as the lightning flashes out of one part under heaven shines to the other part under heaven, so also the Son of Man will be in His day.

John 6:40—The will of God is that all that sees the Son and believes in Him may have everlasting life. and I will raise him up at the last day.

John 14:3—I will come again and receive you to Myself; that where I am, there you may be also.

Acts 1:11—two men in white apparel told those who saw Jesus who was taken up into heaven "This same Jesus who was taken up from you into heaven, will come in like manner as you saw Him go into heaven.

Rom 15:4—Things written before were written for our learning, that we through the patience and comfort grant you to be like minded toward one another.

1 Cor 15:51-54—we shall not all sleep, but we shall all be changed—in a moment, in the twinkling of an eye, at the last trumpet. For the trumpet will sound, and the dead will be raised incorruptible and we shall be changed. For this corruptible must put on incorruption, and this mortal has put on immortality, then shall be brought to pass the saying; "Death is swallowed up in victory.

1 Thess 4:16-17—For the Lord Himself will descend from heaven with a shout, with a voice of an archangel, and with the trumpet of God. And the dead in Christ will rise first. Then we who are alive shall be caught up together with them in the clouds to meet the Lord in the air. And thus we shall always be with the Lord.

1 Thess 5:1-8—The Day of the Lord comes as a thief in the night. For when they say peace and safety! Then sudden destruction comes upon them —they shall not escape. V-9-God did not appoint us to wrath, but to obtain salvation through our Lord Jesus Christ.

2 Thess 1:8-9—in flaming fire taking vengeance on those who do not know God, and on those who do not obey the gospel of our Lord Jesus Christ.—these shall be punished with everlasting destruction from the presence of the Lord and from the glory of His power.

2 Thess 2:9-12—the working of Satan with all power, signs, and lying wonders and with all unrighteous deception among those who perish, because they did not receive the love of the Truth, that they might be saved. and for this reason God will send them strong delusion, that they should believe the lie, that they all may be condemned who did not believe the Truth but had pleasure in unrighteousness.

1 Tim 4:1—in latter times some will depart from the Truth, giving heed to deceiving spirits and doctrines of demons, speaking lies in hypocrisy, having their own conscience seared with a hot iron.

2 Tim 4:8—there is laid up for me the crown of righteousness which the Lord, the righteous Judge will give to me on that day, and not to me only but also to all who have loved His appearing.

2 Peter 3:3-14—scoffers will come in the last days, Walking according to their own lust, and saying. "where is the promise of His coming? but, beloved, do not forget this one thing, that with the Lord one day is as a thousand years and thousand years as a one day." —But the day of the Lord will come as a thief in the night, in which the heavens will pass away with a great noise, and the elements will melt with fervent heat; both the earth and the works that are in it will be burned up.

1 John 2:28—If we abide in Him, we may have confidence and not be ashamed before Him at His coming.

1John 3:3—All who hath this hope [Christ coming] in him purifies himself even as He is pure.

Jude 14-15—Enoch prophesied of the Lord's coming with ten thousand of His angels.

Rev 1:7—Christ comes with clouds and every eye shall see Him, also those that pierced Him.

Rev 2:25—that which we have believed, hold fast till He comes.

Rev 3:3—Christ warns that if we don't watch for His coming, He will come like a thief!

Rev 3:10-11—Behold, I am coming quickly! Hold fast what you have, that no one take your crown.

Rev 14:14-16—Jesus comes sitting on a cloud with a sickle in His hand.

Rev 16:15—Christ will come to those as a thief, who don't watch.

Rev 19:11-16,21—I saw heaven opened, and behold a white horse —he was clothed with a robe dipped in blood, and His name was called "The Word of God." And the armies of heaven followed Him on white horses.

Rev 22"7—Behold, I am coming quickly! Blessed is he who keeps the words of the prophecy of this book.

Rev 22:20-21—Surely I am coming quickly!

"The one thing Satan cannot counterfeit is the manner in which the 'Advent of Christ coming,"

CHAPTER 31

HOW TO BE SAVED

"Believe on the Lord Jesus Christ, and thou shalt be saved, and thy house"—Acts 16:31. This is the reply the apostles gave the jailer, when he ask—V 30—"What must I do to be saved?" All people have sinned and as a result death has crept like a dark shadow over the whole human race. the word Gospel, means good words or good news. It answers that one supremely question, How can man be saved? You say—"What must I do to be saved" I cannot save myself. We cannot change our hearts any more than we can change our skins. The natural heart is contrary to God's Law of righteousness. Because the carnal mind is enmity against God; for it is not subject to the law of God, neither indeed can be—Rom 8:7. We are invited to "behold the Lamb of God, which taketh away the sin of the world."—John 1:29. It is written in Isaiah 45:22; "look unto Me, and be ye saved, all the ends of the earth: for I am God, and there is none else." The best known verse in the Bible is John 3:16. We need to repeat this verse over and over to ourselves. Notice carefully what this text says!

God————————————————————an almighty authority

So loved the world——————————the mightiest motive.

That He gave His only Begotten Son————the greatest Gift.

That whosoever————————————all are welcome

Believeth in Him——————————the easiest escape

Should not perish——————————a divine deliverance

But have everlasting Life—————a priceless possession

Our salvation depends upon the love of God! It is not hard for us to love those who love us, but it is not human to love the unlovely and the hateful. But God commendeth His love toward us, while we were yet sinners, Christ died for us. "Greater love hath no man than this, that a man lay down his life for his friends." John 15:13. But Christ died for His enemies. We see His love, but shall never comprehend it fully here on earth, and it will be the science and song of the redeemed through the endless ages of eternity. to believe on Jesus Christ is to receive Him. John 1:12—but as many as received Him, to them He gave power to become the sons of God, even to them that believe on His name.

Satan says, "Tomorrow will be ok!

God says, "Today."

Satan says, "Another day."

But tomorrow is a day that never comes. it's always today. "Now is the accepted time; now is the day of salvation." 2 Corinthians 6:2.

Noah in such a time as when the world had become so wicked, heard God's word. He acted upon it. He sacrificed time, energy, everything, to build the ark. But was it worth it, for he saved his family and his name is among the heroes of 'faith'!

CHAPTER 32

"CHOICE"—WHAT WILL BE YOUR'S?

GOD CREATED "ANGELS" AND "MANKIND" WITH FREE "CHOICE"!

What would this world be like if mankind did not have free choice? What if the angels did not have free choice, but were mere robots? If mankind and angels did not have free choice and our acts and works were mechanically and without thinking for ourselves, life would be a drudge, a mechanical being without thinking for ourselves. How many people would agree they would like to live where they did not have a choice?

Is it hard to understand why our Lord created mankind as He did, with a mind and the ability to choose for ourselves. Temptation is not sin; the sin lies in yielding. To the soul who trusts in Jesus, temptation means victory and greater strength.

Some today might blame our Creator Lord for the condition of the world today, but God wants all to know about His Love. Every thing God created has been created with Love instilled in their mind. We don't have to look far to see Love in the hearts of animals, and birds and every thing God created has love built in them. Try and rob a bird nest of baby birds, or a bear of her cubs. Even our babies know love soon as they are born.

Why is it so hard for the human families to understand why our Creator God created every thing He created with Love born in them from birth.

We are told in [1 JOHN 4:18-21] "There is no fear in Love, instead, Love drives out fear, because fear involves punishment. We read in God's Book how sin resulted in fear when Adam and Eve sinned in heaven. They hid from God in the garden from God. Think of what is happening around the world today, even the nations of the world live in fear that another nation will harm them. People around the world are living in fear that they will suffer from someone, another person, nation, go hungry, etc. Where is this fear from? From God or Satan? We know that God is Love [1 John 4:8]" He who does not love does not know God, for God is Love." One of my favorite verses in God's Book is [Lam 3:22] "Because of the faithful love we do not perish, for His mercies never end. They are new every morning."

Do we understand better why God created mankind with the ability to choose, with the ability to Love Him by choice and not a robot? [1 John 4:8] "He that loveth not, knoweth not God."

When we know about God, why He created mankind with the ability to love by choice, we also see in our world today what happen's when mankind chooses not to love God and each other. We today are the result of the choice that Eve and Adam made. Only one tree in all Gods creation, Adam and Eve were asked not to touch or eat of. Had Adam and Eve trusted God and not their ability to choose, but to trust God, what might have been?

As Lucifer choose his own way and even one-third of the angels with him, chose not to honor God their Creator, we see today the result of their choice. We today need to trust what God has told us in His Word. If only we could trust God now, what a world of difference we could enjoy. [1John 4:18-21] "There is no fear in Love, perfect love drives out fear, because fear involves punishment.—If anyone says, "I love God" yet hates his brother, he is a liar—the one who loves God must also love his brother."

Why is there today so much hate for one another, and for the leaders of the nations? People today have chosen as did our first parents to love self more than other's and Jesus Christ. Each person has to make their choice, whether to choose the life of Christ as our guide, and be blessed in the end of our life on earth, or live in fear today of what will happen tomorrow. Satan wants us to make his choice, our choice as he did with Adam and Eve in the garden of Eden. No one can make our choice for us. We alone are left alone to make the choice, whether life eternal, where Love rules or the choice which Lucifer made that ends with his and his angels and be destroyed with all who loves sin more than love for God our Creator, who loves us enough to come and suffer and die in our place.

Don't let Satan or anyone make the choice for you. Jesus came to this world and suffered and died for our sins, but left the choice to each person, whether to love as our Creator created us to love or to believe the lies of the greatest deceiver ever! Jesus would have come and suffered and died for the sins of just one person, because He loves His Creation so much and wants to love us much more.

Our Lord is not saving people because they belong to a certain church. he is saving those who love and obey His Law of Love. have you made your choice?

Think about all the families on earth today. Do we or did we have rules for our children or boundaries for each other as married husband and wife? Do you think that our Creator God would create us without guidelines to live by? Who would let their children walk into a roadway of busy traffic? Who would like driving their car on a mountain road without a center lane or guardrail? Would you feel secure driving on the roads where everyone could drive where they pleased? That is the reason we have center lines and guard rails for safety. Do you think our Creator would create man and woman without guidelines to live by? Parents don't do this with our children do we? Why does the world think God created this world without rules or Laws? How many rules did you have for your children? God has only [10] 'Ten' laws for all mankind to honor, but the choice is left up to each person. It's our choice, we are not 'robots', aren't you glad you have a choice? Some people in this world don't know there is a Creator God, and don't know there is a Law for our safety, and that we have a choice to live by God's Law. What a God we have that loves us and will save us if we choose to honor God by obeying His Law and loving as God does! The choice is ours, we are not robots.

Want to be happy, read [Ps 119:1\ and [Prov 28:9]. One who turns away his ear from hearing His Law, even his prayers is an abomination.

Don't you know that heaven will be a happy place! Everyone there will be there because of the choice they made on this earth, because they love our Creator God and all that who will be there will live by the Law of God. We will honor one another, no murdering, no adultery, no stealing, no lies. And [Isa 66:23] "It shall come to pass that from one new moon to another, from one Sabbath to another, all flesh shall come to worship before Me, says the Lord."

For many married couples to have quality time for each other, they schedule a regular "date nite." One nite a week is reserved which they can spend meaningful time together. Life does get busy as we all know, God knew this would become a problem for mankind. Don't you think God knew mankind needed a time to rest and come and have time to spend with Him? God has promised this will go on forever, an eternity when we get to heaven. God has given us an open invitation in Matt 11:28—"Come to Me, all you who are heavy laden, and I will give you rest." At the end of creation week, God set aside a day that would be special time for His people to spend with Him. He gave us the Sabbath Day as a release valve—as protection against the demands of life. How special is this day? [Ezk 46:1] "the Sabbath day is a day for people to refrain from their regular secular pursuits and instead dedicate that time to God. Does it really matter which day I keep as the Sabbath? The Sabbath Day is the Sabbath of the Lord our God. It isn't possible to keep any other day as the Sabbath, because the seventh day is the only day that is Holy.

CHAPTER 33

ARE THERE ANY CHURCHES THAT HONOR THE SABBATH OF CREATION?

To find a list of Sabbath Keeping Churches —Look on line with your computer —"The Bible Sabbath association." Their list is not complete as there are now well over 500 different denominations that have discovered the truth about this forgotten Commandment that was lost in the dark ages, and the list is growing larger by the day.

Some of the largest Sabbath keeping Churches would be the Seventh Day Baptist. Seventh-Day Adventist, Church of God. and the United Church of God. This web site says the 'Seventh-day Adventist Church understands Bible prophecy better than any other of the Churches that have been investigated, but they are attacked by people more fiercely then you can ever imagine, they seem to be deliberate attacks inspired by Satan himself because they prove to be a huge threat to him.

The most accurate of these Churches is the one that has the most criticisms and attacks coming against it. Never underestimate the ability of the enemy to make a Church with the most Biblical truth and the best understanding on Bible Prophecy to be falsely labelled as a cult. It should be obvious to us that Satan will attack truth the hardest and has no trouble finding those he can deceive to accomplish his task very convincingly. To find the most Biblically accurate Church, you will need to personally do your own research and not just read web sites. To find the best and most Biblically accurate Church, you need to personally compare the Scripture's to what is taught. Even this can be challenging as some of the things that you may assume to be wrong may in fact be right. What is Truth, is not always popular and what is popular is not always truth. The Church with the most truth will more than not, be the church with the most people and the people attacking it.

It is interesting that the biggest and most Biblically inaccurate Church, which is none other than "Mystery Babylon" [Rev 17] and a woman riding a beast [A woman in prophecy is a church} that has the blood of millions of Christians saints on her hands, has almost nothing coming against it. Why is this So? "Satan" attacks the church with the most truth. Most people believe these attacks like they do the Gospel truth without researching to find out if they are lies. This church is none other than the Church that changed God's Sabbath to Sunday in favor of Sun worship. You will find that any Sabbath keeping denomination of any significant size will have Satan coming against it. It is important to Satan that he keeps Christians deceived on the truth about the Sabbath especially.

What city on earth "was" the counterfeit of the New Jerusalem by Satan? It was Babylon, the capital city of the Babylonia empire— "Babylon"—was four square, had a river running through it, great palaces, hanging gardens suggesting the— tree of life. Satan tried to use this nation to destroy "Israel". He tried to organize the whole world under one man. This nation went down because everything Satan does has death in it. Satan tried again and again with the Medo-Persia, it failed, next was Greece, it failed, next was Rome—which was Lucifer's fourth attempt to rule the world. Rome tried to destroy the "seed" as a Baby in Bethlehem. After four defeats of Satan's attempts at a world empire, never again will there be a world devil-inspired empire. The next world empire is the empire of Christ Jesus.

God has a true Church on earth but some people say the different churches are just different roads leading to the same place. The churches arose from a more or less common source. Like the spokes of a wheel, though all alike, they get farther and farther apart as they leave their source.

The most famous trial in history is the trial of Jesus Christ! Pontius Pilate sat in the chair of authority. He knew Jesus Christ was not guilty of what He was being accused of. Pilate wanted to free Christ, but wanted to please the people too. Are we different today about how we honor Christ? Do we really want to accept the cross of Christ and be saved? Pilate thought of a plan, he thought he would please the crowd, Barabbas, a robber and murderer was the representative of Satan, whom Pilate thought would be away to excuse and free Christ and save face too. Do you friend realize, that we today stand like the people then, we make the same choice, do we accept Christ or Barabbas. Jesus Christ suffered what Barabbas was guilty of, and Barabbas was set free. Jesus Christ has paid our penalty, for our sins that we can be forgiven. Barabbas represents the condition of all lost people in general, we only need to ask forgiveness and Jesus has paid for all our sins when we commit our lives to Him, and live to help others to know what our God and Saviour has done for those that Love Him. What is your choice? Don't wait, who know's if we will be here tomorrow?

So friend, today the choice is ours. What will it be? Who will it be? Christ or Barabbas? Hope or despair? Make Jesus Christ your King now and forever. You have a right to be there, because Jesus paid your debt. [Rev 22:14] "Blessed are they that do His commandments, that they may have right to the tree of life, and may enter in through the gates into the city." Are you a sinner, open your Bible to [1 Tim 1:15] "This is a faithful saying, and worthy of all acceptation, that Christ Jesus came into the world to save sinners." This verse give each one in this world hope that Jesus Christ wants all to be saved, for all are sinners. We only need to love and honor what Christ has asked and believe what He has said. Love is the answer to all Christ has asked!

God desires man to be happy, and for this reason He gave him the precepts of His law, that in obeying these he might have joy at home and abroad. The fact that Jesus died to bring happiness and heaven within our reach should be a theme for constant gratitude. Love to God and love to our neighbor constitute the whole duty of man. Love is the great controlling power. Our love to God and our love to man will give the clear title to heaven. No one can love God supremely and transgress one of His commandments. There is no power that can close the door of communication between God and man. Neither man nor Satan can close the door which Christ has opened for us. Rev 3:8 "Behold, I set before thee an open door, and no man can shut it."

PURPOSE OF THIS BOOK

The one purpose of this book is that you can understand the relationship our Creator God wants with His children that He has created on this earth. As you have read and discover how far we all have departed from what our Creator made at creation week, we all need to renew our relationship with our Creator God.

My friend, whoever you are and wherever you are, and no matter how far you have gone away from God, this call is for you. Accept Christ's atoning sacrifice for your sins, there on Calvary's cross where the old account was settled years ago! You cannot purchase His Gift, only except His Gift of Love. Soon and very soon, "The Son of Man shall come in the glory of His Father with His angels; and then, He shall reward every man according to his works"—. Matt 16:27. Do you want to be one of those that will hear His voice calling those who Loves Christ? Make your decision today!

Printed in the United States
By Bookmasters